Table of Contents

I. Introduction
- a. Summary 3
- b. Benefits of Sign Language 5
- c. Foreword by Dr. Marilyn Daniels 6
- d. ASL & Alt. Forms of Communication 9
- e. Three Channels of Communication 10
- f. Tips for Signing with Children 12
- g. Developmental Milestones 14
- h. Outcomes & Indicators 17
- i. Stories 23
- j. Songs 25
- k. Games & Activities 26
- l. Crafts 29

II. Signs
- a. Handshapes – a Quick Glance 31
- b. Alphabet – a Quick Glance 32
- c. Alphabet 34
- d. Basic Signs 61
- e. Questions 170

III. Handouts 180

IV. Index 215

Introduction

The Time to Sign Young Children's Themed Curriculum is designed to teach young children, families and educators American Sign Language (ASL). The Young Children's Themed Curriculum covers over 900 age-appropriate signs. Each sign includes a description, the word in Spanish, the word fingerspelled and an illustration of the sign. You will also find information about ASL and other forms of manual communication. We hope you enjoy learning and teaching ASL to your children.

About Time to Sign

Time to Sign is the nation's leader in educational materials and training services for teaching ASL to children of all ages in a fun and engaging way through the use of mnemonics, stories, songs, games and play. Time to Sign's uniquely created and trademarked proprietary products utilize sound developmental principles and practices to teach children, parents, educators and childcare providers how to sign. All of Time to Sign's curriculums, videos, learning guides and resources are the result of painstaking research and exhaustive review by experts in the fields of sign language, deaf educators, speech pathology, audiology and members of the deaf community.

Time to Sign founder Lillian Hubler's workshops and techniques have been featured on numerous media outlets including ABC, CNN, and the Washington Post.

In addition to educational resources, Time to Sign, Inc. conducts workshops and classes for children, families, childcare providers, preschools and schools that complement the content of our products. For information, comments or questions regarding this and other Time to Sign materials please contact us at 321-259-0976 to request a catalog or visit our website at **www.timetosign.com**.

Our Mission

Time to Sign, Inc. is dedicated to enhancing the communication skills, education, and personal growth and development of young children by teaching and using American Sign Language (ASL) in a fun and educational way.

Summary

This Curriculum is designed to give childcare providers a variety of tools to use in the classroom to teach children American Sign Language (ASL). These books includes theory and research on the benefits of signing with children, information about ASL and other forms of manual communication, language developmental milestones, age appropriate signs and activities, over 900 illustrations of signs, and traditional and new songs.

Curriculum Contents

The Curriculum includes the following Time to Sign 7 modules and other related materials:

Modules:

1. Language Arts (Base Module) – Includes Basic Signs, Colors, and Questions signs.
2. Character Signs – Includes Character, Emotions, Feelings, and Manners signs.
3. Community & School – Includes Community, Post Office, Fire & Police, Health Care, Occupations, Common Classroom, Construction, School, Days of the Week, Functional & Directional Signs, Months, and Time & Day signs and phrases.
4. Food, Farm, Garden & Animals – Food, Vegetables, Fruits, Utensils, Meal, Farm, Garden, Zoo & Jungle Animals, and Ocean Animals signs.
5. Family, Home, Holidays & Transportation – Includes Family, Home, Holidays, Pets and Transportation signs.
6. Math, Science & Nature – Numbers, Math, Measurement, Money, Shapes, Sizes, Insects, Science & Nature, Seasons, and Weather signs.
7. Sports, Recreation & Art – Sports, Recreation, and Fine and Performing Arts.

Each module contains songs, games, stories, crafts and other play activities to be used to facilitate the instruction of sign language. Also, each activity list relevant words and outcomes and indicators. Furthermore, all modules have handouts to send home to the parents in English, Spanish and Sign.

Other related materials:

1. Music Book – includes 90 songs in sign, 2 music CD's and an instrumental CD.
2. Curriculum DVD – over 30 songs in sign and common signs for 0-5 year old children.
3. Lesson Plan Guide – Weekly lesson plans for 52 weeks plus holidays.

Time to Sign Instructional Services:

Time to Sign, Inc. conducts workshops and classes for children, families, and childcare providers that are specifically tailored to the materials contained in this Curriculum. We hope you enjoy learning and teaching ASL to your children. For information, comments or questions regarding these materials please contact us at (321) 259-0976 or visit our website at www.timetosign.com.

Classroom Benefits of Sign Language

- Lowers children's noise levels in the classroom
- Reduces need for teachers to raise their voice
- Enables class to support special needs children
- Children pay better attention, they have to look directly at you
- Sign language gets their attention better than the spoken word
- Increased ability to express themselves reduces instances of misbehavior
- Provides children the ability to express emotions
- Increases children's use of manners

Benefits of Signing with Children

- Enhances children's vocabulary and literacy skills
- Enhances fine motor coordination
- Learning a second language makes additional language learning easier
- Raises communication awareness and abilities
- Babies can communicate their pre-verbal wants and needs
- A fun activity for child and parent/caregiver that reduces frustration and enhances bond between child and parent/caregiver
- Enhances children's confidence and self-esteem
- Enables energetic children to better control their behavior
- Sign language is easier for young children to learn than English
- Young children can learn up to 5 different languages concurrently
- 2-sided brain activity that increases brain functioning
    - Visual right brain usage
    - Cognitive second language left brain usage
    - Creates additional connections or synapses in the brain
    - Creates higher IQ levels in children, on average 10-12 points per child

Why Sign with Hearing Children?
By Dr. Marilyn Daniels, Ph.D.

DR. MARILYN DANIELS OFFERS SOME THOUGHTS ABOUT SIGNING

Does this sound familiar? You have a crying baby in your arms. She's Pointing to... what? A teething ring? Rejected. The spoon on the counter? No. The crying escalates. Ah, you think, as you offer every single item in the room if only they could communicate.

Nowadays it is possible to do just that. You can teach your baby to communicate through sign language. Far from simply reducing frustration in the pre-verbal child, itself not a negligible goal, teaching children sign language has additional benefits. Namely increasing their spoken vocabularies, helping them with reading, and improving their linguistic ability in general.

I and researchers in other fields, including psychology, human development, and family science, have independently produced studies demonstrating that infants as young as nine months can learn basic signs, allowing them to communicate with their parents and care givers long before they are verbal. This in turn can reduce parental and infant frustration and help develop a child's self-esteem.

A recent e-mail I received from a former colleague illustrates the point:

> *"Marilyn, I have always been interested in your research regarding teaching sign language to young children. I thought you might be interested to know that in a small way your work has had a neat impact on my family... here's the story. My eldest daughter, Karen, was a communication major at Penn State and attended many Speech Communication Association of Pennsylvania meetings while she was a student. She heard of your work at one of the meetings and she and I discussed it over the years.*
>
> *Karen is now the mother of Emma who is 15 months old. Emma has been able to tell us for about 5 months that she is hungry, wants a drink, wants more of something, and that she is tired because Karen used signs to express those ideas. Em is now trying language - Mom, Dad, shoe, puppy - and still uses her signs to more fully and accurately tell us what she wants. Em also seems to have a true sense of what words are all about and seems to purposefully attempt to attach sounds to concepts. Karen and her husband, Ed, are terrific parents but it seems to my very biased eye that the signing really has helped bypass much of the parent/child frustration that can occur when a child can't get mom or dad to understand their needs.*
>
> *I know this is a tiny adaptation of your scholarly life-work but I thought you might enjoy knowing this. We also find that strangers are fascinated by seeing this little person using her signs to get a drink or another bite of food. So, thanks to you for helping us make our Emma all that much more special.*
>
> *Elaine"*

In a way this is not all new. For many years, we have all shown babies how to wave "bye-bye" and demonstrate "so big", and many educators now belief that sign predated speech in the evolution of human communication. This premise has recently been brought to our attention by the posthumous publication of Dr. William Stokoe's last major work: Language in Hand: Why Sign Came Before Speech, published by Gallaudet University Press in 2001. It is significant that Stokoe, the researcher who is credited with legitimizing American Sign Language (ASL) as a bona fide language, makes this claim in the book, which has been referred to as his intellectual will and testament to the field of study that he started forty years ago.

During the past 15 years I, as well as other researchers, have been focused on systematic efforts to use sign language with children in much the same way we use spoken language with them. We have spawned a new movement: teaching hearing babies and children to use sign language. I have found, as my colleague Elaine describes, sign offers parents and caregivers a unique opportunity to communicate in an effortless way with babies and young children. Further, my research shows hearing children who used sign in their pre kindergarten and kindergarten classes scored better on vocabulary tests and attained higher reading levels than their non-signing peers. The studies of others in this country and the United Kingdom are confirming my results.

Here's why the system works. Babies can learn sign language because they understand symbolic communication before they can form words with their mouths. If you stop to think about it, you will realize that children understand their parents long before their parents understand them. Deaf babies babble with their fingers just as hearing babies babble with their voices, but Deaf children are able to sign months before hearing children can speak. This occurs because they have the motor control to make the signs. The vocal apparatus to form speech develops more slowly than the manual dexterity to form signs.

Using sign language encourages language-delayed and shy children to increase their language acquisition skills in a relatively pressure-free manner. It is difficult for some children to speak well, but with sign the children are on a more level playing field and don't feel inhibited. In addition, children are more attentive simply because they have to be. When you are speaking to someone you don't really have to make eye contact, but when you're using sign language, you naturally and unconsciously focus your attention on the person signing. This improves the quality of the communication.

The added benefits of signing derive in part from its unique status as both a visual and kinetic language. There are individual memory stores for each language a person knows, even at the initial stages of acquiring the second or third language. You intake sign with your eyes, using the right side of the brain. Then like any other language, sign is processed and stored in the brain's left hemisphere. This operation creates more synapses in the brain, adding to its growth and development. It also helps to establish two memory stores in the left hemisphere for language, one for English (or the native language) and one for ASL. So children who use both develop a built-in redundancy of memory, storing the same word in two formats in two places.

Furthermore, because visual cues are taken in with the right side of the brain while language engages the left using ASL activates both sides of the brain at once. In the same way that bilingual children develop greater brain function, users of sign language build more connections or synapses in the brain than those who use English alone and because of the kinetic component of sign language, the ASL brain benefits even more than the bilingual one because of the dual-hemisphere work. Babies using sign language are simply building more brain.

For a more in-depth analysis of this topic I suggest you consult my web site marilyndaniels.com or my book, Dancing with Words, Signing for Hearing Children's Literacy, where you will find additional information. I wish each of you and the children with whom you communicate much success in realizing the benefits of sign language.

Marilyn Daniels, Ph.D.

About Dr. Daniels

Dr. Marilyn Daniels is a Penn State Professor of Speech Communication who publishes books and articles concerning the use of American Sign Language (ASL) with both hearing and Deaf individuals. Her book, Benedictine Roots in the Development in Deaf Education, Listening with the Heart, earned wide acclaim in both the hearing world and the Deaf community. Dr. Daniel's abiding interest is the art of human communication in all its forms. Currently, she focuses on improving communication by enhancing literacy. To this end she has designed and conducted numerous research studies in which hearing children from babyhood through sixth grade use various amounts of sign language to enhance their literacy. Over the past twelve years, Dr. Daniels' amazing results from these endeavors consistently demonstrate how sign language facilitates children's ability to communicate with words.

Dr. Daniels secured her position as the world's foremost authority on the use of sign language with hearing children with Bergin and Garvey's 2001 publication of her latest book, Dancing with Words, Signing for Hearing Children's Literacy. The major thesis of her book is the value ASL offers to hearing children's literacy. Using sign with hearing children helps them see words, feel words, spell words, acquire words, understand words, speak words, read words, and communicate with words. Sign has also been shown to reduce conflict, increase self-esteem, and facilitate an understanding of human emotions. Dr. Daniels recent findings clearly indicate this bilingual approach with hearing children activates brain growth and development.

Marilyn Daniels, Ph.D., Associate Professor, Department of Speech Communication, Penn State University, 120 Ridge View Drive, Dunmore, PA 18512-1699, Office: 570 963-2670 • FAX: 570 963-2535 • Email: mxd34@psu.edu

Seven Things to Know Prior to Signing

1. Dominant Hand: Use to refer to begin and make the sign(s). Use your normally dominant hand as your dominant hand in sign language. If the sign is a one-handed sign, then you use your dominant hand to form the handshape. If you are left- handed then you use your left hand as your dominant signing hand, if preferred. In this text, the right hand is shown as the dominant hand.
2. Reference Hand: Use to support your dominant hand in making the sign(s). In this text, the left hand is shown as the reference hand.
3. Negation: Shake your head "no" as you produce the sign.
4. Affirmation: Nod your head "yes" as you produce the sign.
5. Gender Signs: Male signs are formed in the forehead area, while female signs are formed in the chin area.
6. Facial Expressions: Should support what you are signing. "Your face will surely show it."
7. Person Indicator : The "er". Both hands just inside the shoulder, palms facing each other, hands coming down simultaneously from the shoulders to the waist. Referred to as "agent" sign in this text.

American Sign Language and Alternative Forms of Communication

American Sign Language (ASL)

ASL is a language, used in the U.S. and Canada, which uses no voice. This means that ASL is not derived from English, or any other voiced or spoken language. ASL has its own unique grammar and language structure (or syntax), including: facial grammatical markers, spatial linguistic information, finger spelling, and individual signs. ASL is a true and natural language where the sign often mimics the experiences with ideas or objects.

The six basic components of ASL are: eye contact, facial expressions, body language, mouth, movements, hand movements and signing space.

Signing Essential English (SEE1)

Uses ASL hand signs together with the grammar and syntax rules of spoken Standard English. It is very literal and uses strict English word order. Every article, verb and verb part (e.g., "am & going"), conjunction, preposition, etc., is signed.

Signing Exact English (SEE2)

Very similar to SEE1 except for minor differences. For example, compound words have a different, single sign in SEE2 .SEE1 uses the two separate signs for each word part of the compound word: bedroom.

Signed English

Similar to SEE1 and SEE2, however it uses ASL signs in a more simple, "concept" delivery. Not all words are signed. It does use English word order, but far less "structure." Primarily intended for use with young children and others with limited cognitive skills.

Cued Speech

Uses set of hand shapes (not formal ASL signs) that "add value" to speech-reading. The hand shapes are made at specific locations around the face to help distinguish different sounds that look similar on the lips.

Contact Sign (Pidgin Signed English)

The form in which most hearing people sign to deaf people. Contact Sign (PSE) utilizes ASL signs but in English word order. Most interpreters translate in Contact Sign (PSE).

Three Channels of Communication

Effectively combining the Three Channels of Communication improves communication. Inconsistent use of the can impede the transmission of your message.

1. Body Language (Crossed arms, Eye contact, Smiles, Etc.)
2. Tone and Modulation (Emotion, Volume, Tone, Etc.)
3. Words (Spoken, Written, Listened, Read)

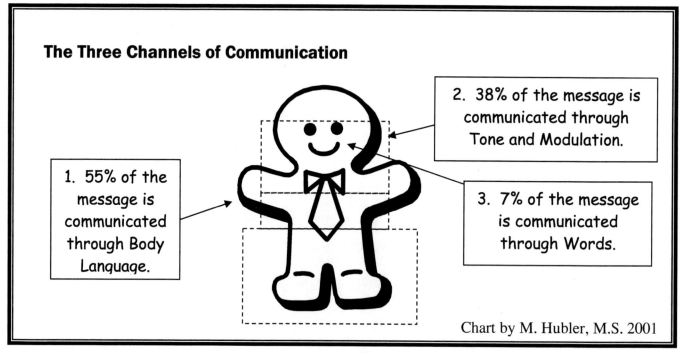

Chart by M. Hubler, M.S. 2001

Improving Communication

Effectively combining the three channels improves communication. Inconsistent use of the Three Channels of Communication can impede the transmission of your message.

Emphatic Listening

Emphatic Listening is a form of active listening that allows you to identify with and understand the person you are communicating with emotionally and intellectually. Empathic listening fosters meaningful communication and creates close relationships.

When using Emphatic Listening, you are able to listen to, and comprehend the speaker's frame of reference. With Emphatic Listening, the meaning of what the speaker is saying, their ideas and what they think is important are much clearer to you. You will also be more aware of non-verbal communication and the subtext of the conversation. Consequently, the speaker senses your comprehension and feels invited to tell their story and release their feelings.

In using Emphatic listening, you are more likely to use appropriate tone and modulation with your own voice and select the correct words to communicate.

Communication Information

In Context
Children are perpetually "in the moment." For learning to occur, it must be connected or associated to a current event. For example, just prior to offering more milk, use the signs for "more milk." Repeated, consistent use of a sign in context will allow children to begin making the connection on their own. Then they will try to imitate the sign themselves. Eventually, they'll respond to your signs for "more milk" by gesturing or signing "yes" or "no."

Eye Contact and Gazes
Use these opportunities to focus children's attention on some person/object/event ***and*** you at the same time, wait a moment, introduce (or repeat) a sign, say the word while signing it at the sight line between you and the child. This provides the "context" to "associate" learning and "make meaning."

Gazes
Expressive Gaze: Children look at you to communicate wants, needs, thoughts, or feelings
Chance Mutual Gaze: Children's eyes and your eyes meet without intent or particular reason
Pointed Gaze: Some event or sound causes a child and you to first look in the same direction for its source (person/thing/event) – Next, you both turn and look at each other

Hints for Effective Communication
Establish Rapport
Communicate Openly and Honestly
Listen Empathically
Be Specific About What You Want or Need
Give and Receive Positive Feedback
Use "I" Phrases

Methods for Teaching and Use of Sign Language in the Classroom
Hand over Hand
Games or Activities
Songs
Transitions
Crafts

Signing with Children

When are children ready to sign?

- When children attain enough motor coordination they will begin to respond.

- When children have been exposed to a sign on a daily basis and have had time to practice processing its meaning.

- When children demonstrate an active desire to communicate – pointing, vocalizing with tone & modulation (babbling or jabbering sounds; conversational or inquisitive), grunting while pointing at object/person, and other attempts at physical or visual cues to get attention or to enlist assistance.

Getting started: Using sign language with children

- You can begin signing with your child at birth. Start with some key basic signs to meet children's wants and needs. For example you should begin with signs such as: eat, more, drink, please, and milk.

- Begin with one or two signs then work your way up to a few more. Don't be discouraged if your child seemingly doesn't notice your signs. Be consistent! One day the children will simply produce their first signs.

- As you see the children begin to use their first few signs regularly, begin introducing additional signs. Be sure to observe children's cues, and practice introducing signs slowly, clearly, and in context.

- Children learn best when everyone who is caring for them uses the same signs the same way. "Mixed-message" signs can frustrate children. Repetition and consistency are the key factors for children's learning.

When is the "Best" time to teach sign language?

- **"Quiet Alert" State** – Infants in this state provide a lot of pleasure and positive feedback for caregivers. It is the best time to provide infants with stimulation and learning opportunities. In this state children will display the following characteristics:

  - Minimal body activity
  - Brightening and widening of eyes
  - Faces have bright, shining, sparkling looks
  - Regular breathing pattern
  - Curious about their environment, focusing attention on any stimuli that are present

- **In context** –Children are perpetually *"in the moment."* For learning to occur, it must be connected or associated to a current event. For example, just prior to offering more milk (bottle or nursing), use the signs for "more milk." Repeated, consistent use of a sign in context will allow children to begin making the connection on their own. Then they will try to imitate the sign themselves. Eventually, they'll respond to your signs for "more milk" by gesturing or signing "yes" or "no."

Eye "Gaze" Contact – Use these opportunities to focus children's attention on some person/object/event **and** you at the same time, wait a moment, introduce (or repeat) a sign, say the word while signing it at the sight line between you and the child. This provides the "context" to "associate" learning and "make meaning."

Incorporating American Sign language into your daily routine

- Learn the signs for some of the traditional songs that you sing with your children.
- Use common signs with infants, particularly during feeding times to help them learn to communicate while they are pre-verbal. Words such as eat, milk, more, drink, hurt, cold, and hot are easy to sign and particularly useful for the pre-verbal child.
- Sign the alphabet.
- Sign the numbers throughout the day (circle time, head counts, lunch counts).
- Sign the names of the foods at mealtimes.
- Teach children to sign the colors and encourage them to use both the sign and the word when naming colors.
- Teach the children to fingerspell their names.
- Teach the children signs for common actions: eat, play, sing, jump, walk and dance.
- Reduce aggression in your classroom by teaching children signs emotions and manner signs, and signs for common words that they can use if they get frustrated or angry: no, stop, mine, and help. This will reduce the noise level in the classroom as well.
- Teach the children how to sign the names of animals that you discuss in your classroom.
- Use the signs for words commonly used during daily interactions with children such as: Mommy, Daddy, work, home.
- Teach the children to sign "potty" when they need to use the restroom. This will help to reduce the number of interruptions you experience during the day.
- Teachers can use non-verbal cues such a "no" or "stop" across the classroom without having to raise their voices or interrupt a conversation.

Developmental Milestones in Communication

Birth to 6 Months

- Crying is primary form of communication
- Responds to sound
- Vocalizes sounds – gurgling and cooing
- Follows objects
- Smiles and laughs
- Recognizes faces and scents
- Coos when you talk to them
- Prefers human faces to all other patterns and colors
- Can distinguish between bold colors
- Amuses themselves by playing with hands and feet
- Turns toward sounds and voices
- Imitates sounds, blows bubbles
- Squeals
- Recognizes own name

7 to 12 Months

- Imitates speech sounds – babbles
- Says "dada" and "mama"
- Combines syllables into word-like sounds
- Waves "bye-bye"
- Plays pat-a-cake
- Imitates others' activities
- Produces word-like sounds
- Indicates wants with gestures
- Responds to name and understands "no"
- Begins to say additional word or two – other than "mama" and "dada"
- Understands and responds to simple instructions
- Sits without support

13 to 18 Months

- Uses two words skillfully – e.g., "hi", "bye"
- Imitates others
- Vocabulary increases, uses words more often
- Turns the pages of a book
- Enjoys pretend games
- Will "read" board books on his own
- Scribbles well
- Enjoys gazing at their reflection
- Plays "peek-a-boo"
- Points to one body part when asked
- Adopts "no" as their favorite word
- Responds to directions – "Sit down"
- Speaks more clearly
- Strings words together in phrases

Copyright © 2008 Time to Sign, Inc.

Language Arts

19 to 24 Months
- Recognizes when something is stated incorrectly – e.g. someone calls a cat a dog
- Learns words at a rate of 10 or more a day
- Searches for hidden objects
- Follows two-step requests – "Get your toy and bring it here"
- Can name a simple picture in a book
- Can use 50 single words
- Half of speech is understandable
- Produces short sentences
- Capable of identifying several body parts
- Produces two or three word sentences
- Sings simple tunes
- Begins talking about self

25 to 30 Months
- Names several body parts
- Speaks clearly most to all of the time
- Understands emotional expressions
- Answers "wh" questions
- Uses up to 200 words
- Asks simple questions
- Comprehends up to 500 words
- Listens to a 5-10 minute story

31 to 36 Months
- Names six or more body parts
- Names one color
- Carries on conversations of two to three sentences
- Describes how two objects are used
- Uses four to five words in a sentence
- Uses prepositions – on, in, over
- Follows a two or three part command
- Uses up to 500 words
- Comprehends up to 900 words
- Listens to 10 minute story
- Understands simple comparisons – big/little
- Repeats common rhymes

37 to 42 Months

- Engages in longer dialogue
- Requests permission – "May I?"
- Corrects others when they misspeak
- Clarifies own conversation when misunderstood
- Uses up to 800 words
- Answers simple "how" questions
- Uses compound sentences with "and"
- Comprehends 1,200 words
- Emerging understanding of location – "in front of", "behind"
- Recognizes simple comparisons – hard/soft, rough/smooth
- Recognizes the names of simple shapes – circle, square

43 to 48 Months

- Speech is more fluid and understandable
- Uses up to 1,000 – 1,500 words
- Comprehends up to 1,500 – 2,000 words
- Begins to understand the difference between fiction/non-fiction
- Uses more details in conversation
- Emerging ability to accurately discuss topics/events, e.g. "out of context"
- Effectively uses vocabulary to express personal thoughts – discusses emotions and feelings
- Narrative and retelling skills – able to tell and sequence story or situation events, emerging understanding of characters and character development
- Emerging use of conjunctions – "because"
- Emerging use of reflexive pronouns – "myself"

49 to 60 Months

- Connected speech and language understandable
- Uses "what do…does…did" questions
- Uses 1,500 to 2,000 words
- Answers simple "when" questions
- Retells long story with increasing accuracy
- Knows and can state full name – first, middle, last
- Reflexive pronouns emerging more consistently
- Comparatives vs. superlatives emerging – "-er," "-est"
- Uses 5 to 8 word sentences
- Developing understanding of prepositions – between, above, below, bottom
- Repeats the days of the week
- Emerging ability to name months – knows birthday (day and month)

Language Arts  17

Outcomes & Indicators

The Child Outcomes and indicators are depicted as follows:

Domain
    Domain Element
         Indicators

A. Language Development

A.1 Listening & Understanding

- A.1.a. Sign language naturally demonstrates increased ability to understand and participate in conversations, stories, songs, rhythms, and games
- A.1.b. Sign language assists in the understanding and following of simple and multiple-step directions
- A.1.c. Sign language greatly increases children's receptive vocabulary
- A.1.d. Sign language assists non-English-speaking children in learning to listen to and understand English as well sign language

A.2 Speaking & Communication

- A.2.a. Sign language assists in developing increasing abilities to understand and use sign language and English to communicate information, experiences, ideas, feelings, opinions, needs, and questions for other purposes
- A.2.b. Sign language instruction teaches children the use of an increasingly complex and varied signed and spoken vocabulary
- A.2.c. Sign language assists non-English speaking children in signing and speaking English

B. Literacy

B.1 Phonological Awareness

As teachers say and sign words together it serves as another way for children to understand and remember both the sign and the spoken word. When taught together sign instruction assists in providing the following benefits.

- B.1.a. Progresses in recognizing matching sounds in familiar words, songs, rhythms, games, stories, and other activities
- B.1.b. Associates sounds with written and signed words
- B.1.c. Children's use of sign language enhances language acquisition
- B.1.d. Children's learning of sign language simultaneously with words assist in like word differentiation of emergent readers

B.2 Book Knowledge & Appreciation

- B.2.a. Signing is an enjoyable activity for children that greatly enhances vocabulary, which makes learning to read easier and sometimes earlier
- B.2.b. Children who are taught sign language demonstrate progress in abilities to retell, using sign words, stories from books and personal experiences
- B.2.c. Children who are taught sign language demonstrate progress in abilities to act out stories in dramatic play which is a natural extension of the hand and finger movements learned in sign language

B.3 Print Awareness and Concepts

- B.3.a. Children who learn to sign develop a growing understanding of the different functions of forms of print such as signs, letters, and numbers
- B.3.b. When written words are presented with the verbal and sign introduction/instruction children better learn to recognize a word as a unit of print

B.4 Early Writing

- B.4.a. Begins to represent stories and experiences through signs, pictures, songs, games, and in play

B.5 Alphabet Knowledge

- B.5.a. Shows progress in associating the names of letters with their signs, shapes, and sounds
- B.5.b. Identifies all the letters of the alphabet, especially those in their own name
- B.5.c. Knows that the letters of the alphabet are a special category of visual graphics that can be individually signed and named

C. Mathematics

C.1 Number & Operations

- C.1.a. Children are taught the sign language counterparts to the numbers
- C.1.b. Children count numbers to assist with the retention of the number they have reached
- C.1.c. Signing assists with children's ability to count beyond the number 10
- C.1.d. Signing assists with children's learning to make use of one-to-one correspondence in counting objects and matching numbers of groups of objects

C.2 Geometry & Spatial Sense

- C.2.a. Signing assists with the recognition and ability to describe common shapes as shape signs accurately represent common shapes such as square, triangle, or circle
- C.2.b Signing assists children in developing visual and spatial awareness

D. Science

D.1 Scientific Skills & Methods

- D.1.a. Signing assists children in the understanding of scientific principles such as being able to express differences (such as big/little, open/closed, and more/less)
- D.1.b. Signing assists in increasing children's awareness
- D.1.c. Singing assists in the growing awareness of ideas and language related to time

D.2 Scientific Knowledge

- D.2.a. Signing assists in increasing awareness and beginning understanding of changes in material and cause-effect relationships
- D.2.b. Signing assists in increasing awareness of ideas and language related to time and temperature
- D.2.c. Signing assists in expanding knowledge of and respect for their body and the environment
- D.2.d. Signing enhances children's abilities to observe, describe and discuss the natural world, materials, living things, and natural processes

E. Creative Arts

E.1 Music

- E.1.a. As children sign to music they develop increased interest and enjoyment in
- listening, singing, signing, finger plays, games, and performances

E.2 Movement

- E.2.a. Children express through sign what is felt and heard in music

E.3 Dramatic Play

- E.3.a. Children express themselves dramatically through signing

F. Social & Development

F.1 Self Concept

- F.1.a. Begins to develop and express awareness of self in terms of specific abilities, characteristics and preferences through the use of signing, for example they learn to sign their name and are given a sign name they feel reflects their personality
- F.1.b. Children's successful use of sign language enhances their confidence and self-esteem

F.2 Self Control

- F.2.a. Through the use of sign language children learn to express their feelings, emotions, needs, and opinions in everyday and in difficult situations without harming themselves, others, or property
- F.2.b. Through the use of sign language children demonstrate increased capacity to follows rules and routines, and to use materials purposefully, safely and respectfully
- F.2.c. Children's use of sign language raises communication awareness, enabling them to better tell and understand how their actions and words effect others
- F.2.d. Children's and teacher's use of sign language lowers children's noise levels in the classroom enhancing the learning atmosphere
- F.2.e. Children's use of sign language teaches them to pay better attention, they need to pay attention visually, rather than just listen
- F.2.f. Children's use of sign language increase their use of manners, which can help to eliminate potential misbehavior reactions
- F.2.g Children's use of sign language fosters an atmosphere in which children ask questions before acting, for example asking if their classmate is done with the toy before taking it and angering their classmate
- F.2.h. Classroom usage of sign language engages the teachers to be present with the child, they need to be making regular eye contact and can better see in the faces of children if anything is wrong, the child is unhappy, etc.

F.3 Cooperation

- F.3.a. Children's use of sign language increases their abilities to sustain interactions with peers through the use of manners, enabling them to express their feelings and emotions, by helping, and by sharing
- F.3.b. Children's use of sign language increases their abilities to use compromise and discussion in playing and resolving conflicts with classmates
- F.3.c. Children's use of sign language increases their abilities to give and take in interactions; to take turns in games or using materials; and to be participatory in activities while not being overly aggressive

F.4 Social Relationships

- F.4.a. Children's use of sign language increases their signing and speaking with and accepting guidance and directions from a wide range of familiar adults
- F.4.b. Children and teacher's use of sign language in the classroom enables all in the classroom to develop friendships with peers, this is particularly true and key for any special needs members of the class. Without sign language it can be difficult, or impossible, for enough communication to be established to enable special needs children to build necessary friendships to insure a successful social development. Many special needs children drop-out of programs for this very reason
- F.4.c. Children's use of sign language teaches them to be especially aware when classmates are in need, upset, hurt, or angry; and in expressing empathy for others

F.5 Knowledge of Families & Communities

- F.5.a. The Young Children's Signing Program incorporates family signs to assist in children's understanding of family composition
- F.5.b. The Young Children's Signing Program incorporates gender signs, boy and girl, to assist in children's understanding of genders

G. Approaches to Learning

G.1 Initiative & Curiosity

- G.1.a. Children's use of sign language increases participation in an increasing variety of tasks and activities
- G.1.b. Children's use of sign language enhances their use of imagination and inventiveness in participation in tasks and activities

G.2 Engagement & Persistence

- G.2.a Children's learning of sign language also assist them as they increase their capacity to maintain concentration over time on a task, question, or set of directions or interactions

G.3 Reasoning & Problem Solving

- G.3.a. Children's learning and use of sign language assists in the recognition and problem solving through active exploration, including trial and error, and interactions and discussions with classmates and adults

H. Physical Health & Development

H.1. Fine Motor Skills

- H.1 a. Children's learning of sign language develops hand and arm strength and dexterity needed to control such instruments as a hammer, scissors, tape, and a stapler
- H.1.b. Children's learning of sign language develops hand-eye coordination required for use of building blocks, putting puzzles together, reproducing shapes and patterns, stringing beads, and using scissors
- H.1.c. Children's learning of sign language develops drawing and art tools such as pencils, crayons, markers, chalk, paint brushes, and computers
- H.1.d. Children's learning of sign language enables them to be able to pick up small objects

H.2 Gross Motor Skills

- H.2.a. Children's learning of sign language coordinates movements in throwing, catching, and bouncing balls

H.3 Health Status & Practices

- H.3.a. Children's learning of sign language enhances their ability to communicate health and hygiene problems to adults
- H.3.b. Children's learning of sign language enhances their knowledge of health and hygiene

Language Arts

Stories

Brown Bear by Bill Martin Jr. & Eric Carle (colors, animals, teddy bear)
Topical signs to be learned: brown, bear, what, you, see, red, bird, blue, horse, black, sheep, gold, fish, purple, cat, green, frog, yellow, duck, white, dog, teacher, children, all/everyone.

Indicators: A.1.a, A.1.b, A.1.c, A.1.d, A.2.a, A.2.b, A.2.c, B.1.a, B.1.e, B.2.a, B.2.b, B.2.c, B.2.c, B.3.a, B.4.a, H.1.a, and H.1.b

Baby Faces (DK Publishing)
Topical signs to be learned: happy, sad, puzzled, surprised, where's baby, peek-a-boo, angry, worried, crying, laughing, hungry, kiss, dirty, clean, tired, fast asleep.

Indicators: A.1.a, A.1.b, A.1.c, A.1.d, A.2.a, A.2.b, A.2.c, B.1.a, B.1.e, B.2.a, B.2.b, B.2.c, B.2.c, B.3.a, B.4.a, H.1.a, and H.1.b

Brown Rabbit's Shape Book by Alan Baker (colors, shapes)
Topical signs to be learned: Brown, rabbit, red, triangle, shape, rectangle, square, box, underneath, inside, circle, five, flat, balloons, different, colors, big, round, orange, oval, egg, away, flew, green, long, purple, smaller, pear, long, curly.

Indicators: A.1.a, A.1.b, A.1.c, A.1.d, A.2.a, A.2.b, A.2.c, B.1.a, B.1.e, B.2.a, B.2.b, B.2.c, B.2.c, B.3.a, B.4.a, H.1.a, and H.1.b

Colorful Tiger Time to Sign Book by Elisabeth Nichols, Illustrated by Brian Miller (shapes) Topical signs to be learned: colors, tiger, far, away,

Indicators: A.1.a, A.1.b, A.1.c, A.1.d, A.2.a, A.2.b, A.2.c, B.1.a, B.1.e, B.2.a, B.2.b, B.2.c, B.2.c, B.3.a, B.4.a, H.1.a, and H.1.b

Little Blue & Little Yellow by Leo Lioni (colors, family)
Topical signs to be learned: little, blue, yellow, papa, mama, many, friends, best, play, hide and seek, "Ring around the Rosie", sit, rows, school, run, jump, looked, here, there, everywhere, hugged, green, ran, chased, orange, climbed, mountain, tired, cried.

Indicators: A.1.a, A.1.b, A.1.c, A.1.d, A.2.a, A.2.b, A.2.c, B.1.a, B.1.e, B.2.a, B.2.b, B.2.c, B.2.c, B.3.a, B.4.a, H.1.a, and H.1.b

My Five Senses by Alika
Topical signs to be learned: see, hear, smell, touch, senses, five, sun, frog, my, baby, sister, drum, fire engine, bird, soap, tree, cookies, oven, drink, milk, eat, food, cat (kitten), balloon, water, laugh, play, dog (puppy), bounce, ball, four, three.

Indicators: A.1.a, A.1.b, A.1.c, A.1.d, A.2.a, A.2.b, A.2.c, B.1.a, B.1.e, B.2.a, B.2.b, B.2.c, B.2.c, B.3.a, B.4.a, H.1.a, and H.1.b

Language Arts

Say It, Sign It by Elaine Epstein
Topical signs to be learned: water, pretty, boat, great, snake, grandpa, my, car, grandma, fun.

Indicators: A.1.a, A.1.b, A.1.c, A.1.d, A.2.a, A.2.b, A.2.c, B.1.a, B.1.e, B.2.a, B.2.b, B.2.c, B.2.c, B.3.a, B.4.a, H.1.a, and H.1.b

Today I Feel Silly And Other Moods That Make My Day by Jamie Lee Curtis
Topical signs to be learned: silly, mood, bad, grumpy, mean, angry, today, feelings, hurt, joyful, confused, glad, quiet, understands, cried, excited, cranky, lonely, happy, great, discouraged, frustrated, sad, frown, face, great, best, inside, ok, "How do you feel Today?"

Indicators: A.1.a, A.1.b, A.1.c, A.1.d, A.2.a, A.2.b, A.2.c, B.1.a, B.1.e, B.2.a, B.2.b, B.2.c, B.2.c, B.3.a, B.4.a, H.1.a, and H.1.b

White Rabbit's Color Book by Alan Baker (colors)
Topical signs to be learned: white, rabbit, three, tubs, paint, red, yellow, blue, sunshine, lovely, bright, sun, white, orange, look, together, make, time, wash, hot, cool, purple, important, princess, shower, icy, cold, warm, no more, water, brown, just, right, for, me.

Indicators: A.1.a, A.1.b, A.1.c, A.1.d, A.2.a, A.2.b, A.2.c, B.1.a, B.1.e, B.2.a, B.2.b, B.2.c, B.2.c, B.3.a, B.4.a, H.1.a, and H.1.b

White Rabbit's Color Book by Alan Baker (colors)
Topical signs to be learned: white, rabbit, three, tubs, paint, red, yellow, blue, sunshine, lovely, bright, sun, white, orange, look, together, make, time, wash, hot, cool, purple, important, princess, shower, icy, cold, warm, no more, water, brown, just, right, for, me.

Indicators: A.1.a, A.1.b, A.1.c, A.1.d, A.2.a, A.2.b, A.2.c, B.1.a, B.1.e, B.2.a, B.2.b, B.2.c, B.2.c, B.3.a, B.4.a, H.1.a, and H.1.b

Songs

ABC Song – (general) . . . . Toddler-Preschool Music Book

Can You Find – (colors) . . . . Language Arts Song Section

Five Senses Song, The – (general) . . . . Toddler-Preschool Music Book

If You're Happy And You Know It – (emotions) . . . . Infant-Toddler Music Book

I'm A Little Bubble (general) . . . . Language Arts Song Section

I'm A Little Teapot (general) . . . . Language Arts Song Section

Make New Friends – (general) . . . . Toddler-Preschool Music Book

March and Sing (general) . . . . Language Arts Song Section

More We Sign Together, The – (general) . . . . Preschool-School Age Music Book

Muffin Man – (general) . . . . Infant-Toddler Music Book

Mulberry Bush – (general) . . . . Preschool-School Age Music Book

She'll be Coming 'Round the Mountain – (general) . . Preschool-School Age Music Book

Tell Me Why – (emotions) . . . . Preschool-School Age Music Book

Touch Your Nose (general) . . . . Language Arts Song Section

Where Is Thumbkin? – (general) . . . . Infant-Toddler Music Book

You are My Sunshine – (emotions) . . . . Toddler-Preschool Music Book

Games & Activities

Brown Bear
Make Flannel board pieces for the story, and then tell it using the pieces. Once children have become familiar with the story, introduce animal signs. Retell the story by giving each child an animal and having them place it on the flannel board as you tell the story but sign the animal. Repeat process by adding color signs. Once children have mastered animals, colors and the story, retell it by signing and having the children place pieces on the flannel board in the correct order. For a change of pace, the teacher can hold onto the pieces and have the children retell the story by signing colors and animals. The teacher then has to place correct pieces on the flannel board. Have fun with it and let them correct you, after all we need to let them know we all make mistakes!
Indicators: A.1.c, A.1.d, A.2.a, A.2.b, A.2.c, G.1.a, G.2.a, H.1.a, and H.1.b

Colors
Circle game. Use the color cards to help teach the children the signs for colors. Have the children take turns telling you the color then show them the sign. The color signs can be reused again and again to reinforce the learning of colors and their signs.
Indicators: A.1.c, A.1.d, A.2.a, A.2.b, A.2.c, G.1.a, G.2.a, H.1.a, and H.1.b

Color Games I
Have the children sit with you in a circle. Teach/review the color signs that make up your rainbow. Have the children repeat all the signs to the leader as they are demonstrated. Children each select, or are assigned, a color. The children take turns going around the circle clockwise demonstrating the sign for their chosen color. The leader begins the game by signing their color then that of another person. The person they have 'called', signs their sign then that of another in the circle. In about 5 minutes they should have learned all the color signs. Assist anyone who needs help with the signs, especially the last to go to insure they succeed. Praise the children for their success.
Indicators: A.1.c, A.1.d, A.2.a, A.2.b, A.2.c, G.1.a, G.2.a, H.1.a, and H.1.b

Color Games II
Have the children sit with you in a circle. Teach/review the color signs for the various items to be picked up off the floor, as well as please and thank you. Have the children repeat all the signs to the leader as they are demonstrated. Go around the circle having each child take a turn picking an item out of the center of the circle. They sign the color of the item and then place it in the box/bag. (The teacher signs 'thank you' each time a child places an item in the bag/box.) In the first round, have all the children sign the appropriate color sign for every item put away. In the second round, have only the child whose turn it is sign the color. Assist anyone who needs help with the signs to insure success. End the game by having everyone do the rainbow sign together. Additional rounds: add the name of the item as well as the color. Assist anyone who needs help with the signs, especially the last to go to insure they succeed. Praise the children for their success.
Indicators: A.1.c, A.1.d, A.2.a, A.2.b, A.2.c, G.1.a, G.2.a, H.1.a, and H.1.b

Language Arts

Color Games III
Have the children sit with you in a circle. Show the children the colors and rainbow sign cards to teach/review the color signs that make up your rainbow. Have the children repeat all the signs to the leader as they are demonstrated. The children take turns going around the circle clockwise selecting a sign card and showing it to the other children. They display the sign shown on the chosen card. The children take turns going around the circle until all the cards have been used up. (If there are more children than colors, then the cards are placed back in the pile in the middle of the circle for reuse.) End the game by having all the children go through the color signs once again and finish with the rainbow sign. In about 5 minutes they should have learned all the color signs. Assist anyone who needs help with the signs, especially the last to go to insure they succeed. Praise the children for their success.
Indicators: A.1.c, A.1.d, A.2.a, A.2.b, A.2.c, G.1.a, G.2.a, H.1.a, and H.1.b

Color Games IV
Have the children sit with you in a circle. Show the children the colors and rainbow sign cards to teach/review the color signs that make up your rainbow. Have the children repeat all the signs to the leader as they are demonstrated. The children take turns going around the circle clockwise selecting a sign card and showing it to the other children. They create the sign they just picked and the sign(s) of the other children who have already gone. For example, the first person selects red, so she makes the red sign. The second person selects blue. So they do the red and blue signs. And so on. (If there are more children than colors, then the cards are placed back in the pile in the middle of the circle for reuse.) End the game by having all the children go through the color signs once again as they were selected and finish with the rainbow sign. In about 5 minutes they should have learned all the color signs. Assist anyone who needs help with the signs, especially the last to go to insure they succeed. Praise the children for their success.
Indicators: A.1.c, A.1.d, A.2.a, A.2.b, A.2.c, G.1.a, G.2.a, H.1.a, and H.1.b

Color Games V
Either you have an even amount of children or the leader has to play so that everyone has a partner. Start by playing any of the Games 1-4 Rainbow Color Games. When done, have the children pick a color card slip. They have to be quite during this phase of the game. When the leader says go, they will have to make their selected color's sign. Without talking they have to find the others who have the same color. The game ends when they get together with all their same color sign partners and make the rainbow sign. Assist anyone who needs help with the signs or finding their group to insure success. Praise the children for their signing.
Indicators: A.1.c, A.1.d, A.2.a, A.2.b, A.2.c, G.1.a, G.2.a, H.1.a, and H.1.b

Colors, Let's Look At Colors
Play "Find me the color…" and sign the color you want the children to find.
Indicators: A.1.c, A.1.d, A.2.a, A.2.b, A.2.c, G.1.a, G.2.a, H.1.a, and H.1.b

Color Vote
Review color signs they previously learned and have them "vote" for their favorite color. To vote, they need to sign their favorite color sign. When everyone has voted, graph results and help the children determine a winner! Materials: color pictures and signs, and graph of colors.
Indicators: A.1.c, A.1.d, A.2.a, A.2.b, A.2.c, G.1.a, G.2.a, H.1.a, and H.1.b

Emotions Game
Circle game. Teach the children the different emotions signs using the emotions cards. Once they are familiar with the signs, read or make up statements that would refer to one of the emotions. Have the children do the sign for the emotion.
    Example: I dropped my ice cream. I got a new toy. I got a boo boo.
After you, the teacher, go through a few examples have the children think of an emotion to sign and then have them develop a sentence/statement using the word/sign.
This activity helps them learn to express their emotions in a positive manner through the use of sign language.
Indicators: A.1.c, A.1.d, A.2.a, A.2.b, A.2.c, F.2.a, F.2.c, G.1.a, G.2.a, H.1.a, and H.1.b

Feelings Felt Board – (emotions)
Make a simple felt body with a face. The body should look similar to that of a gingerbread man. Make several circular faces that fit the body. Each face should portray a different feeling. Put the body and all the faces on the felt board. Have the children come up one at a time to choose the appropriate face for the emotion signed. Have the child tell when/why they had similar feelings. Have all the children form each of the signed emotions together as a group.
Indicators: A.1.c, A.1.d, A.2.a, A.2.b, A.2.c, F.2.a, F.2.c, G.1.a, G.2.a, H.1.a, and H.1.b

Jumping Jelly Beans
Here is an idea for teaching colors in a most delicious way; with jelly beans! Jelly beans come in a variety of colors and are wonderful for introducing children to colors. Let each child take a jelly bean. Have each child hold up their jelly bean when you name or sign its color. Once each child is sure of their bean's color, have them eat it! As each different color word is substituted, encourage the children who ate a bean of that color to stand up and rub their tummies. Materials: jellybeans.
Indicators: A.1.c, A.1.d, A.2.a, A.2.b, A.2.c, G.1.a, G.2.a, H.1.a, and H.1.b

Who Feels Happy At School Today? – (emotions)
Who feels happy at school today?
All who do clap your hands this way (clap).
Who feels happy at school today?
All who do wink your eyes this way (wink).
Who feels happy at school today?
All who do jump in the air this way (jump).
Indicators: A.1.c, A.1.d, A.2.a, A.2.b, A.2.c, F.2.a, F.2.c, G.1.a, G.2.a, H.1.a, and H.1.b

Crafts

Alphabet Soup Name Bracelet – (alphabet)
It's fun to make name bracelets out of alphabet egg noodles. Spell out your name with some uncooked noodles. Then cut out a small narrow strip of thin cardboard, just big enough to fit your name on. Paste the letters of your name on this strip. When the paste is dry, paint the whole bracelet with poster paint. Carefully poke a hole at each end of the bracelet and pas a small string through both ends. Just slip the name bracelet on your wrist and tie the two ends together. You can make name bracelets for your friends too.
Materials: egg noodles, cardboard, glue, paint, string
Indicators: A.1.a, A.1.b, A.1.c, A.1.d, A.2.a, A.2.b, A.2.c, F.2.b, F.4.a., G.1.a, and G.2.a

Chalk and Sandpaper Letters - (alphabet)
Preparations: Cut sandpaper into desired sizes and pour water into containers. Have the children dip colored chalk into water and then draw designs on the sandpaper. Encourage them to use several different colors.
Materials: Sandpaper of different textures cut into different letters, shallow containers, water.
Indicators: A.1.a, A.1.b, A.1.c, A.1.d, A.2.a, A.2.b, A.2.c, F.2.b, F.4.a., G.1.a, and G.2.a

Colors Book (colors)
Each month designate a page to decorate with pictures and/or items pertaining to the color of the month. You can also use "baggies" for items that cannot be glued into the book.
Materials: white construction paper, collage items and/or pictures depicting the color of the month. Have children bring in a picture from home to go into the book.
Indicators: A.1.a, A.1.b, A.1.c, A.1.d, A.2.a, A.2.b, A.2.c, F.2.b, F.4.a., G.1.a, and G.2.a

Crayon Etching (colors)
Fill the paper with heavy blotches of crayon or a crayon design. Color heavily over the whole paper with black crayon. Plan a picture or design. You might sketch it on scrap paper first. Use a sharp object to scratch the design on the black crayon. The black will come off and the colors will show through wherever you scratch. Try scratching sharp lines and larger areas too. Gently polish the picture to finish it. Use another piece of paper, a tissue, or a paper towel for polishing.
Materials: paper, tagboard, or paper plates (any shape), crayons, nail or un-bent paper clip
Indicators: A.1.a, A.1.b, A.1.c, A.1.d, A.2.a, A.2.b, A.2.c, F.2.b, F.4.a., G.1.a, and G.2.a

Crayon Scratching (colors)
Color a design on the white paper with various colors of crayons. Color darkly. After the page is covered with color, color over the whole thing with black crayon. Press down hard so all of the other colors are covered by the black. Use the paper clip or pen to scratch out your own fireworks display!

Materials: crayons of various colors, one must be black, white paper, paper clip or used up pen.

Indicators: A.1.a, A.1.b, A.1.c, A.1.d, A.2.a, A.2.b, A.2.c, F.2.b, F.4.a., G.1.a, and G.2.a

Lacing Letters - (alphabet)
Make a twelve-inch cardboard set of several letters. Punch holes in the outline of each letter about one inch apart. Attach a two-foot piece of yarn to the letter. Allow children to lace the outline of the letter.
Materials: cardboard, scissors, single hole punch, yarn
Indicators: A.1.a, A.1.b, A.1.c, A.1.d, A.2.a, A.2.b, A.2.c, F.2.b, F.4.a., G.1.a, and G.2.a

Pretzel Letters - (alphabet)
Prepare pretzel dough:
1 1/2 cups warm water 1 envelope of yeast
4 cups flour 1 tsp. salt
Mix all ingredients
Give each of the children enough dough to shape into the first letter of their name. Brush dough letters with beaten egg and sprinkle with coarse salt.
Bake at 425 degrees for twelve minutes.
Materials: water, yeast, flour, salt, egg, egg beater, oven

Secondary Colors (colors)
Have children paint using the three primary colors. Demonstrate how colors are formed, then allow them to experiment.
Materials: tag board, red, yellow and blue paint, and smocks.
Indicators: A.1.a, A.1.b, A.1.c, A.1.d, A.2.a, A.2.b, A.2.c, F.2.b, F.4.a., G.1.a, and G.2.a

Texture Collage – (basic vocabulary)
Have children bring in items that have different textures. Glue items to a piece of cardboard or display board and have children sign back to you what textures are.
Materials: Colored construction paper, glue, water, plastic cup, paint brush, and tissue paper.
Indicators: A.1.a, A.1.b, A.1.c, A.1.d, A.2.a, A.2.b, A.2.c, F.2.b, F.4.a., G.1.a, and G.2.a

Language Arts

Handshapes

bent

bent-V

curved-3

curved-5

flattened-C

flattened-O

modified-C

modified-X

open

Copyright © 2008 Time to Sign, Inc.

Alphabet I

Aa	✊	Gg	👉
Bb	✋	Hh	👉
Cc	🤏	Ii	☝
Dd	☝	Jj	🤙
Ee	✊	Kk	✌
Ff	👌	Ll	🤟

Alphabet II

Mm		Tt	
Nn		Uu	
Oo		Vv	
Pp		Ww	
Qq		Xx	
Rr		Yy	
Ss		Zz	

Alphabet Signs - Señales del Alfabeto

Language Arts

Aa

Bb

Language Arts

Cc

Dd

Language Arts

Ee

Ff

Language Arts 41

Gg

Hh

Language Arts  43

Ii

Jj

Language Arts

Kk

Ll

Language Arts  47

Mm

Nn

Oo

Pp

Language Arts  53

Ss

Copyright © 2008 Time to Sign, Inc.

Tt

Language Arts

Uu

Vv

Language Arts

Ww

Xx

Language Arts

Yy

Zz

Language Arts Basic Signs

Señales del Lenguaje

Language Arts

Move the dominant open hand from the reference shoulder in a large circle in front of the chest, ending with the back of the dominant hand in the reference open hand, palms facing in.

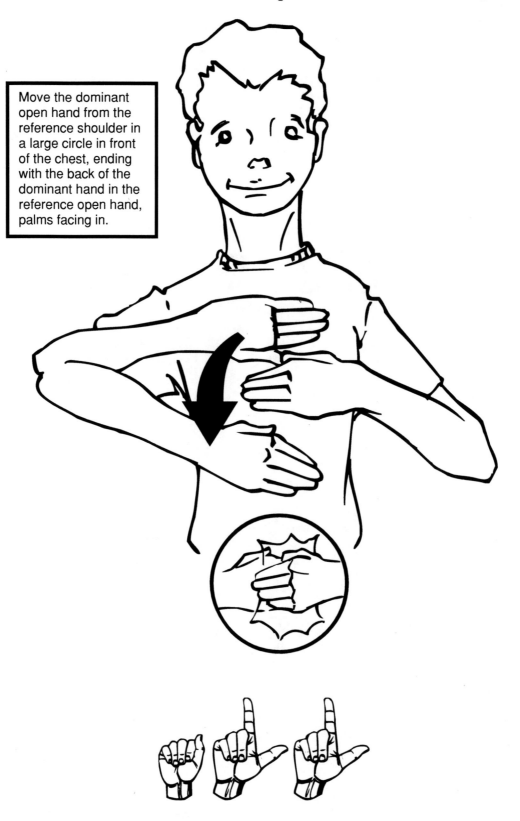

all - todo

Language Arts

Move the dominant index finger in and out of the five fingers of the reference "5" handshape with both palms facing in.

among – entre

Move the extended dominant hand index finger, pointing down, in a small circle around the extended reference hand index finger, pointing up in front of the chest.

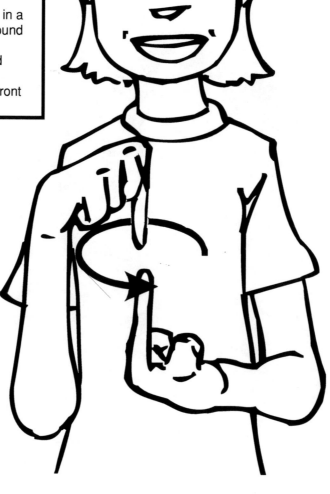

around - alrededor

Language Arts

Flip the fingers of the dominant open hand from pointing down near the dominant side of the body outward by flicking the wrist quickly to the dominant side.

[Natural gesture to shoo something away]

away - lejos

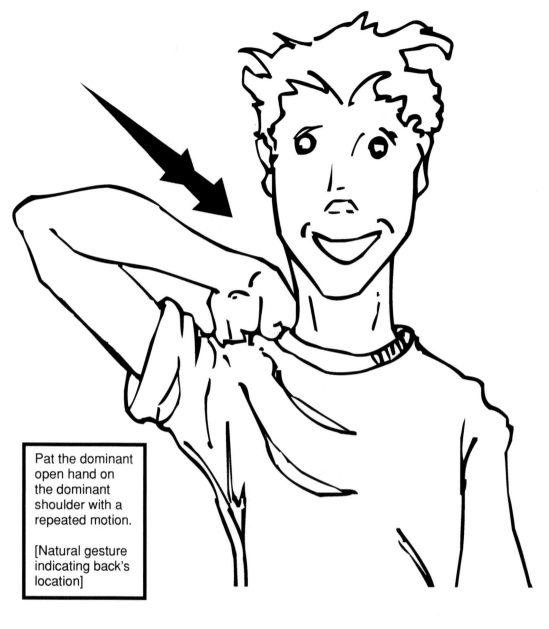

Pat the dominant open hand on the dominant shoulder with a repeated motion.

[Natural gesture indicating back's location]

back – espalda

Language Arts

67

Touch the fingertips of both curved "5" handshape together in front of the chest, palms facing each other.

[Indicates holding a ball in your hands]

ball - pelota

Copyright © 2008 Time to Sign, Inc.

Start with the reference hand fingers cupped over the dominant "S" handshape, held near the mouth, moving both hands apart, with both hands becoming curved "5" handshape, palms facing each other.

[Mimics blowing up a balloon]

balloon – globo

Language Arts

Start with the extended dominant index-finger, palm facing in, inserted in between the index and middle-fingers of the reference hand, palm facing the dominant side and fingers pointing forward. Twist the dominant hand back, ending with the palm angled forward.

[Indicates turning a key to start the ignition]

begin, start - empezar, comenzar

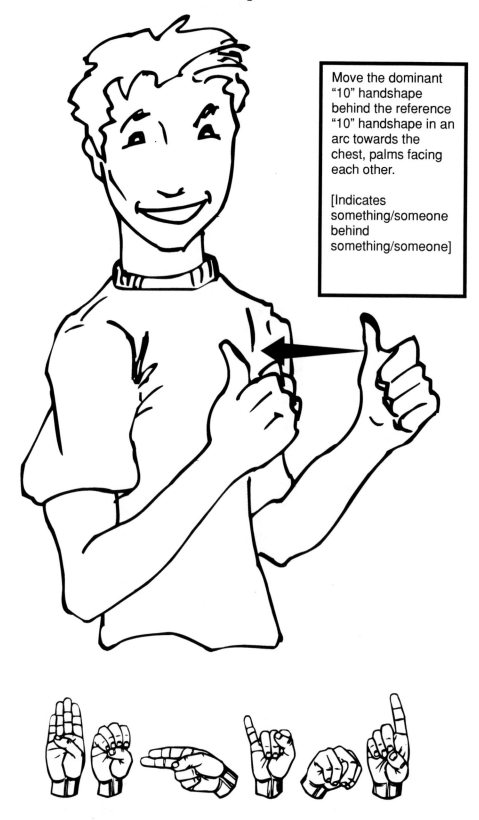

Move the dominant "10" handshape behind the reference "10" handshape in an arc towards the chest, palms facing each other.

[Indicates something/someone behind something/someone]

behind - detrás

Language Arts

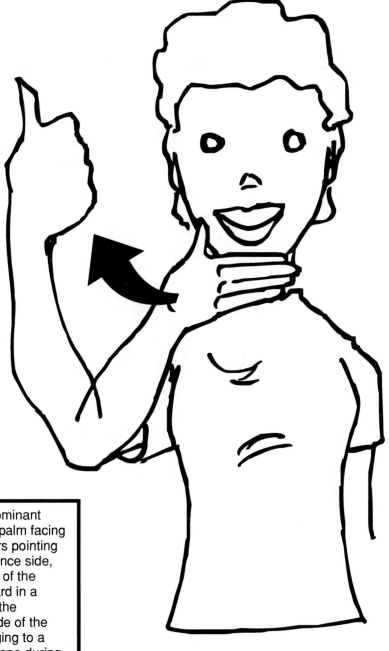

Move the dominant open hand, palm facing in and fingers pointing to the reference side, from in front of the mouth upward in a large arc to the dominant side of the head, changing to a "10" handshape during the arc.

best - mejor

Bring the fingertips of the dominant "C" handshape, palm facing down; down to close around the index-finger side of the reference open hand, palm facing in.

[Indicates teeth biting something]

bite - mordida

Language Arts

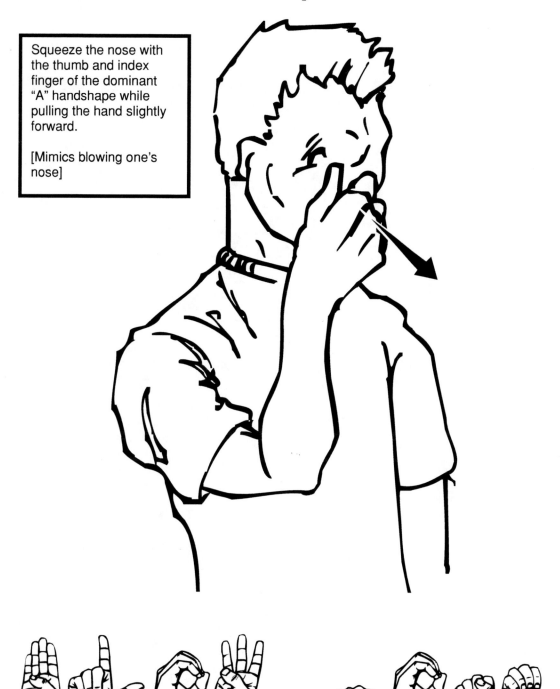

Squeeze the nose with the thumb and index finger of the dominant "A" handshape while pulling the hand slightly forward.

[Mimics blowing one's nose]

blow nose – soplar la nariz

Move the dominant open hand, palm facing down, up and down to the side of the body in a repeated movement.

[Mimics bouncing a ball]

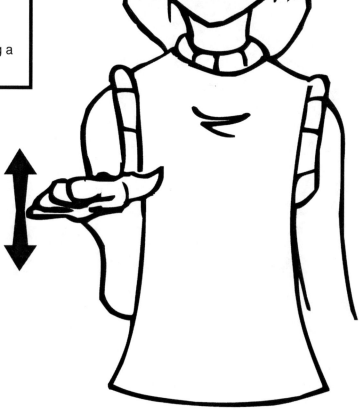

bounce - rebotar

Language Arts

Start with both "S" handshapes in front of the body, index-fingers touching and palms facing down move the hands away from each other while twisting the wrists, ending with the palms facing each other.

[Mimics breaking something]

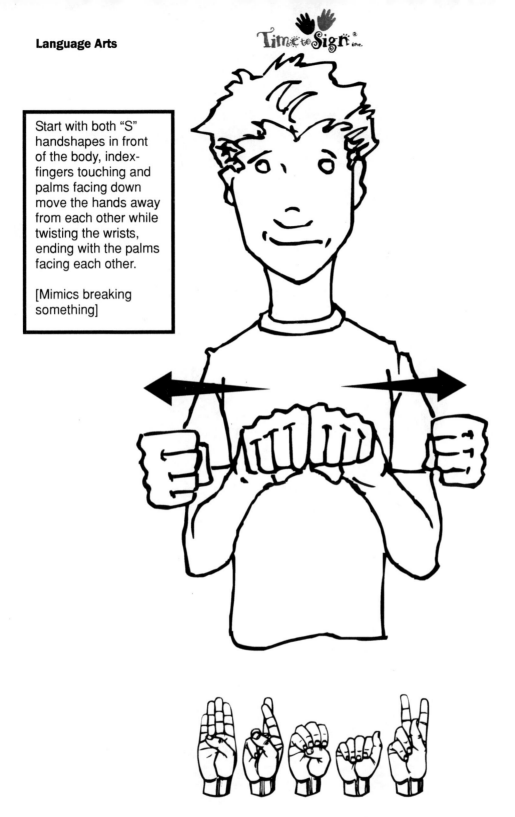

break - romper

Move the palm of the dominant "A" handshape down the dominant side of the head in a repeated movement.

[Mimics brushing of the hair]

brush hair - cepillar el cabello

Language Arts

Move the dominant hand with the index-finger pointed out, palm facing reference side, up and down slightly in front of the teeth..

[Mimics brushing of the teeth]

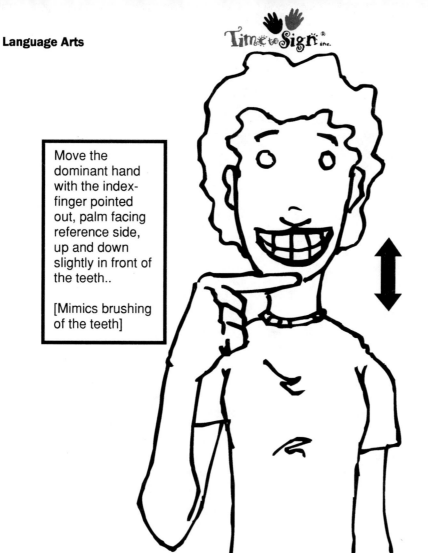

brush teeth – cepillar los dientes

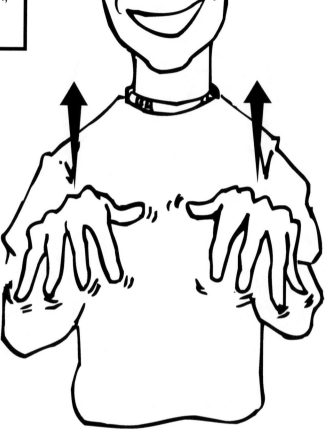

Wiggle the fingers of both curved "5" handshapes, palms facing down and in, while moving the hands slightly up.

bubbles - burbujas

Language Arts

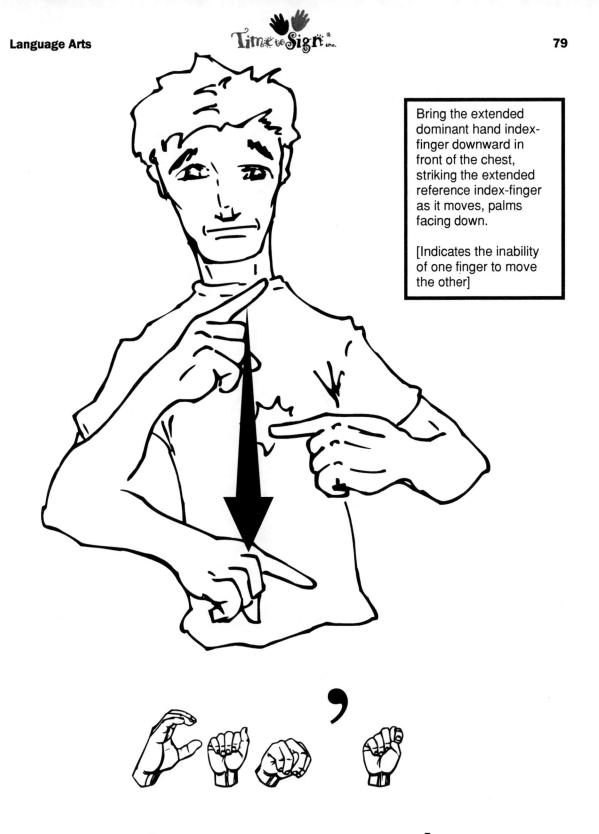

Bring the extended dominant hand index-finger downward in front of the chest, striking the extended reference index-finger as it moves, palms facing down.

[Indicates the inability of one finger to move the other]

can't – no poder

Start with both curved hands, palms facing up, on the dominant side of the body, move the hands in a serious of slight arcs to the reference side of the body.

[Indicates having something in one's hands to transfer from one place to another]

[Also: bring]

carry - llevar

Language Arts

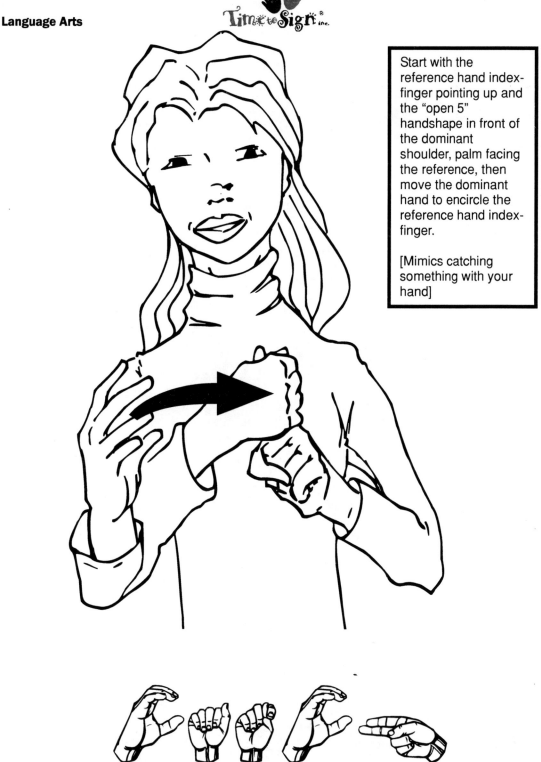

Start with the reference hand index-finger pointing up and the "open 5" handshape in front of the dominant shoulder, palm facing the reference, then move the dominant hand to encircle the reference hand index-finger.

[Mimics catching something with your hand]

catch - coger

With the palm sides of both "X" handshapes together, dominant hand above reference hand, twist the wrists in opposite directions in order to reverse positions.

[Also: adjust, adapt]

change – cambiar

Language Arts

Bring the thumbs of both "A" handshape from near each shoulder, palms facing in, downward and toward each other, ending near the waist.

[Indicates a coat's lapels]

coat - abrigo

Language Arts

Clasp both curved hands together in front of the body, and shake them with a repeated movement, as hands are moved slightly forward.

congratulations - felicitacíones

Language Arts 85

Swing the fingers of the dominant "V" handshape, palm facing in and fingers pointing down, back and forth over the upturned reference hand with a double movement.

[As if dancing with the fingers]

dance – bailar

86

Begin with both "U" handshapes on either side of the waist, palms facing in, bend and unbend the middle and index fingers with a double movement.

Language Arts

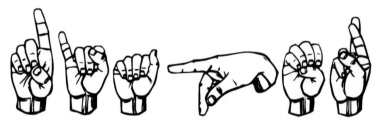

diaper – pañal

Copyright © 2008 Time to Sign, Inc.

Language Arts

With the back of the dominant open hand, under the chin, palm facing down, wiggle the fingers.

dirty - sucio

Language Arts

Move both "C" handshapes, palms facing down, from side to side in front of the body with a repeated movement.

do - hacer

Language Arts

Starting with both open hands crossed in front of the chest, palms angled in opposite directions, move the hands downward away from each other, ending at each side of the body, palms facing down.

don't – no hacer

Move the "1" handshape from the temple outward, while bending the index finger, palm facing in.

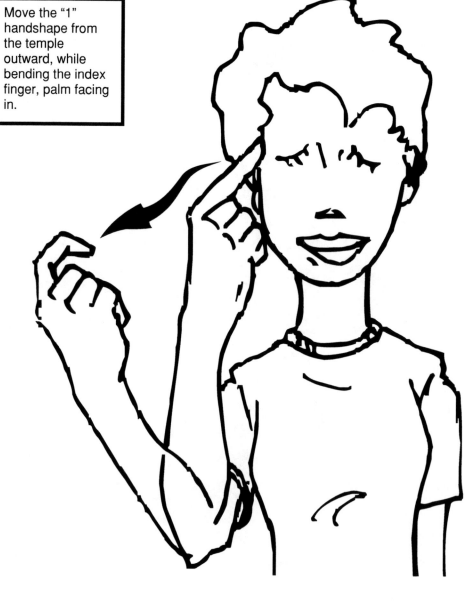

dream – soñar

Language Arts

Start with both flattened "O" handshapes in front of the body, palms facing in and fingers pointing toward each other, drop the fingers of both hands downward while opening into "5" handshapes, ending with both palms facing in and fingers pointing down.

[Mimics something being dropped]

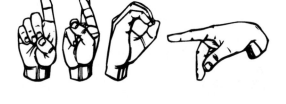

drop – caer

Language Arts

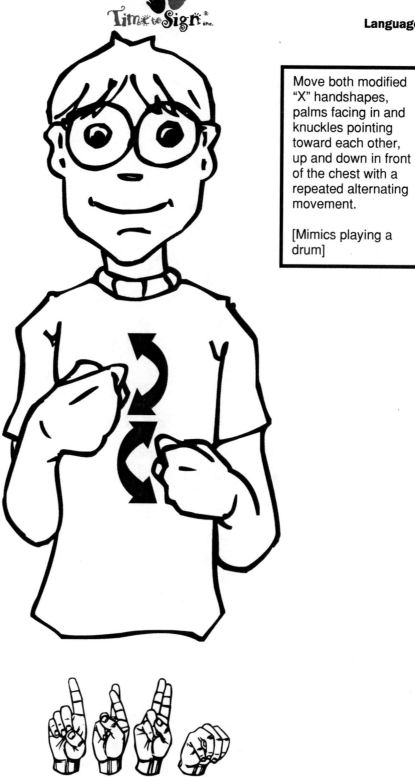

Move both modified "X" handshapes, palms facing in and knuckles pointing toward each other, up and down in front of the chest with a repeated alternating movement.

[Mimics playing a drum]

drum – tambor

Language Arts

Begin with the fingers of both "F" handshapes in front of the chest, palms facing each other and index fingers pointing forward, move the hands forward and back with an alternating movement.

[Also: describe]

explain - explicar

Language Arts

Draw a large circle around the face with the extended dominant hand index finger, palm facing in.

face – cara

Language Arts

Start with the fingertips of the dominant "V" handshape pointing down, palm facing in, touching the upturned palm of the reference open hand. Flip the dominant hand over, ending with the back of the dominant "V" handshape lying across the reference palm.

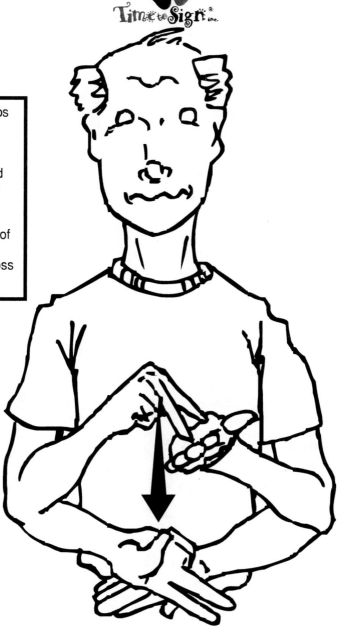

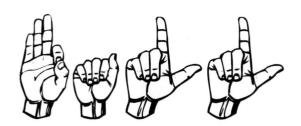 

fall down – caer

Language Arts

Start with the palm sides of both "A" handshapes together in front of the chest, move the dominant hand upwards and forward in a large arc.

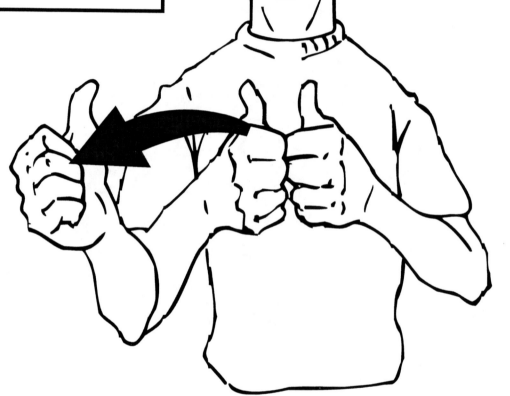

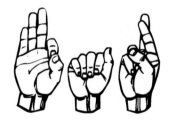

far - lejos

Language Arts

Starting with both extended index-fingers pointing forward in front of the body, palms facing one another; pull the hands quickly back towards the chest while constricting the index fingers into "X" handshapes.

fast, quick – rápido

Language Arts

Starting with both "S" handshapes in front of each shoulder, palms facing each other, then bring hands in with a deliberate movement, ending with wrists crossed in front of the chest.

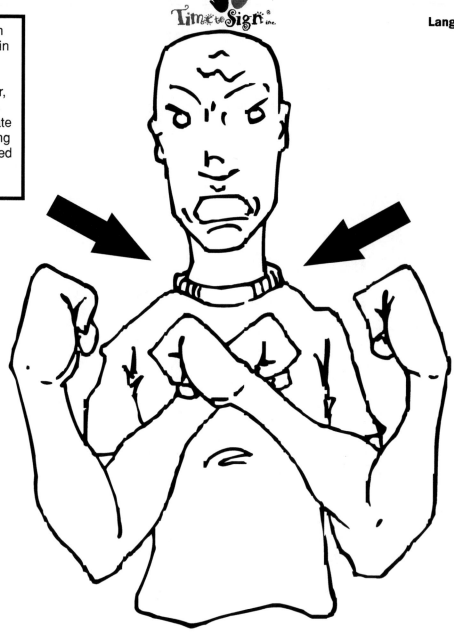

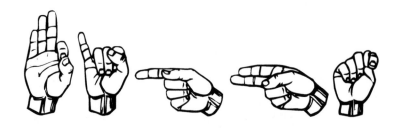

fight – pelea

Language Arts

Hold both "5" handshapes in front of the chest, palms facing in and fingers pointing up, quickly

finish – acabar

Language Arts

Start with the fingers of the dominant "H" handshape touching the end of the nose and the reference "H" handshape in front of the body; bring the dominant "H" handshape downward from the nose to rest on top of the reference "H" handshape, palms facing down.

fun - divertido

Language Arts 101

Starts with both curved "5" handshapes in front of the chest, palms facing up, bring the hands down with a double movement, while closing the hands so the thumbs are touching the fingers.

gentle – gentil, amable

Move both open hands in front of the body, palms facing in and fingers pointing toward each other, forward a short distance simultaneously.

[Mimics pushing something forward]

go on - continuar

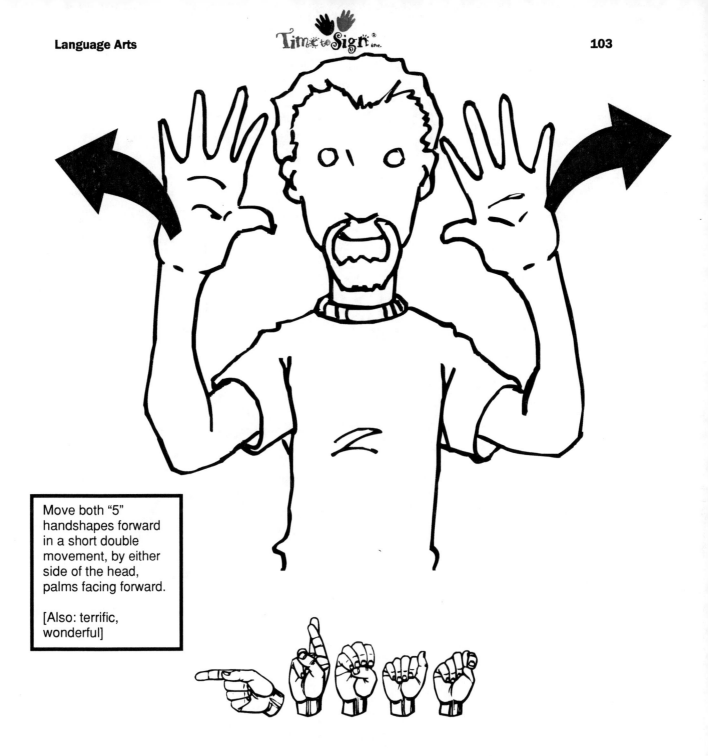

Language Arts

Start with both "G" handshapes in front of the chest, palms facing one another; bring the hands away from each other in outward arcs while turning the palms in ending with the little fingers almost touching and palms facing in.

group - grupo

Language Arts

With both bent "V" handshapes, palms facing in opposite directions, dominant above reference, move the dominant hand down, striking the fingers of the reference hand.

hard - duro

Language Arts

Start with bringing in the fingertips of both bent hands, palms facing in, back to touch each side of the chest.

have - tener

Language Arts

Point the extended dominant index-finger towards the person being referred to.

[This is a directional sign toward the person referred to]

her – ella, him – él, you – tú

Start with both curved hands in front of each side of the body, palms facing up, move the hands towards each other in repeated flat circles.

[Hands are indicating a location near oneself]

here – aquí

Language Arts 109

Push the open dominant hand, palm facing forward, at an angle forward in front of the dominant hand side of the body.

[This is a directional sign toward the person referred to]

hers – suya, his –suyo, yours - tuyo

Language Arts

Move the thumb of the dominant "A" handshape, palm facing reference, from near the mouth in an arc to underneath the reference curved hand, held in front of the chest, palm facing down.

[This motion shows something under the other hand as if to hide it]

hide – escondido

Language Arts

Point the extended dominant index finger to the center of the chest.

I/me – yo/mi

Move the dominant bent "V" handshape, palm facing down, from in front of the dominant side of the body upward and forward in an arc, ending with the hand facing to the dominant side.

journey – viaje

Language Arts 113

Place the dominant "V" handshape in a standing position on the reference palm; lift the "V" handshape, bending the knuckles, and return to a standing position.

[Showing a jumping motion with your fingers]

jump – saltar

Language Arts

Start with the dominant flattened "O" handshape above the dominant shoulder, palm facing down, open the fingers into a "5" handshape.

[Also: shine]

light – luz

Language Arts

Move the dominant "Y" handshape, palm facing forward, from side to side with a double movement.

[Also: similar]

like – similar

Language Arts

Begin with the dominant "S" handshape on top of the reference "S" handshape, palms facing opposite directions, twist the writs in opposite directions with a small, quick, grinding movement.

[As if making something with your hands]

make – hacer

Language Arts 117

Start with both "S" handshapes in front of each side of the chest, palms facing up; open the fingers quickly in a double movement, opening the hands to "5" handshapes.

Begin with both "4" handshapes in front of the body, palms facing in and fingers pointing down, flip the fingers forward and back with a double movement by bending the wrist.

[The hands represent people moving forward in a procession]

march - marchar

Start with the extended index fingers of both hands pointing upwards in front of each respective shoulder, palms facing one another, move the hands together until they touch/meet.

meet – conocer

Language Arts

Place the palm of the dominant open hand on the chest, fingers pointing toward the reference side.

mine, my – mío

120 Language Arts

Start with the dominant hand away from the body, palm facing in, in front of the chest, move this hand to the palm of the reference hand which is out and in front of the same shoulder.

[Also: close]

near - cerca

Language Arts

Touch the middle finger side of the "H" handshape on top of the index finger side of the reference "H" handshape.

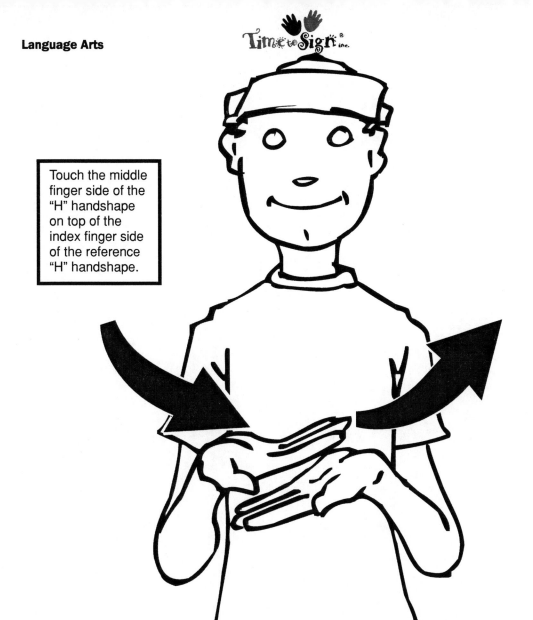

new – nuevo

Touch the extended dominant index finger to the dominant hand side of the nose, palm facing down.

[Body signs are shown by touching the body part]

nose – nariz

Language Arts

Bring the extended thumb of the dominant "10" handshape from under the chin, palm facing reference, forward with a quick movement.

not – no

Bring the palm of the dominant hand upward from the back of the open reference hand held in front of the body, palms facing down.

off - quitar

Language Arts

Start with the dominant "C" handshape near the chin, move the hand downward changing the handshape to an "S".

old – viejo

Bring the palm of the dominant hand downward on the back of the open reference hand held in front of the body, palms facing down.

on - encima

Language Arts

Start with the dominant "10" handshape in front of the body, palm facing down; twist the hand upward to the dominant side, ending with the palm facing up and the extended thumb pointing down.

others – otros

Begin with the fingertips of the dominant bent handshape on the fingertips of the reference bent handshape, palms facing each other and fingers pointing opposite directions, bring the dominant hand upward a short distance in a small arc.

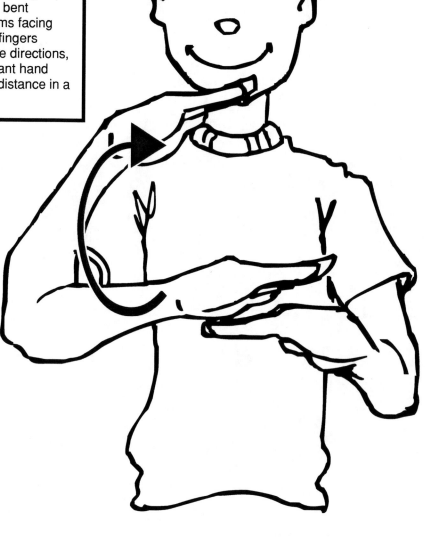

over – por encima

Language Arts 129

Begin with both "A" handshapes in front of the body, palms facing in opposite directions and the reference hand somewhat forward of the dominant hand, move the dominant hand forward, striking the knuckles of the references hand as it passes.

passed – pasar

Language Arts

Start with both open hands covering the eyes, palms facing in and fingers pointing up, turn the hands outward ending with palms facing forward to the sides of the head.

[As if playing peek-a-boo]

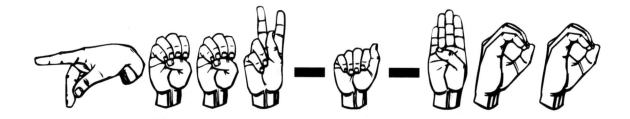

peek-a-boo – juego de esconderse

Language Arts

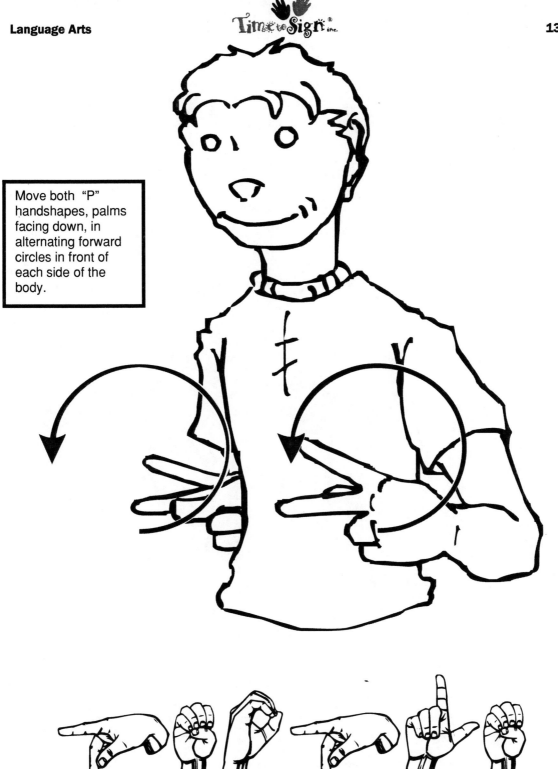

Move both "P" handshapes, palms facing down, in alternating forward circles in front of each side of the body.

people – gente

Language Arts

> Bring both "P" handshapes, palms facing each other, down along the sides of the body with a parallel movement.

person – persona

Language Arts

133

Swing both "Y" handshapes up and down by twisting the wrists in front of each side of the body with a repeated movement.

[Play as in recreation]

play – jugar

Copyright © 2008 Time to Sign, Inc.

Start with the dominant "5" handshape in front of the face, palm facing in, move in a circular movement, closing the fingers and the thumb in front of the chin to form a flattened "O" handshape.

pretty – bonito (a)

Language Arts

Start with both bent "V" handshapes in front of the body, dominant hand placed slightly higher than the reference, palms facing in, alternate moving the dominant hand down and reference hand up, slightly touching the knuckles as they pass.

[Also: difficult]

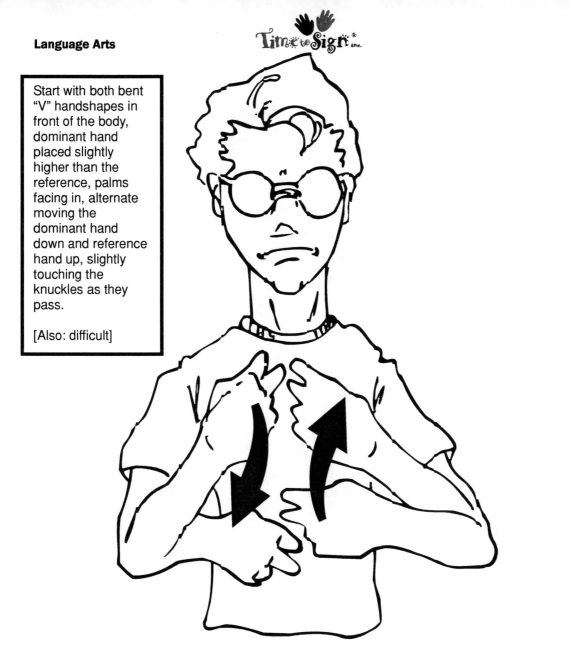

problem - problema

Language Arts

Place the index finger against the mouth.

[As if to make the "shhh" sound]

quiet - quieto, silencio

Language Arts

137

Start with moving both "R" handshapes in front of the reference side of the body, palm facing each other and fingers pointing forward, in a smooth movement to in front of the dominant side of the body.

ready – listo

Move the fingertips of the dominant "5" curved handshape, palm facing down, from the heel to the fingertips of the upturned reference open hand.

rough – áspero

Language Arts

Move the extended dominant index finger, palm facing reference side and finger pointing up, from between the index and middle fingers of the reference "5" handshape, palm facing down in front of the chest, forward with a deliberate movement.

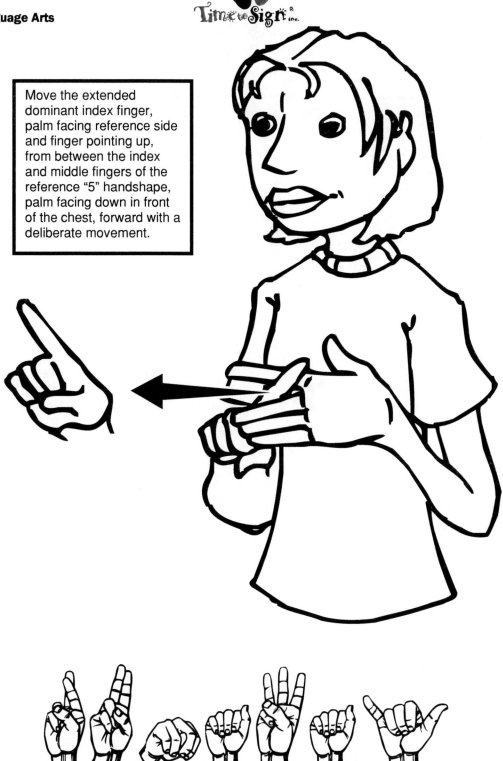

runaway – huir

Move the index finger, held in front of the mouth, forward towards the person being addressed.

[Also: speak, say, tell, speech]

said – dijo

Language Arts

Start with the fingers of the dominant "C" handshape close to the mouth, palm facing in, bring the hand up and out in an arc.

[Also: roar]

don't scream
Simply shake your head no while doing the scream sign.

scream – gritar

Language Arts

Move the dominant "C" handshape, palm facing reference side, with a double movement in a circle in front of the face.

search – buscar

Language Arts 143

Bring the fingers of the dominant "V" handshape from pointing at the eyes, palm facing in, forward a short distance.

see – ver

Language Arts

Start with the bent middle finger of the dominant "5" handshape, palms facing down, touching the back of the open reference handshape, palm facing down, bring the dominant hand upward in front of the chest with a wiggly movement.

shine – brillar

Language Arts

Tap the index finger sides of both "S" handshapes together in front of the chest with a double movement, palms facing down.

shoes – zapatos

Language Arts

Place the tip of the dominant index finger, palm facing in, into the open reference hand, palm facing forward, move both hands forward.

[Also: reveal, for example]

show - mostrar, enseñar

Language Arts 147

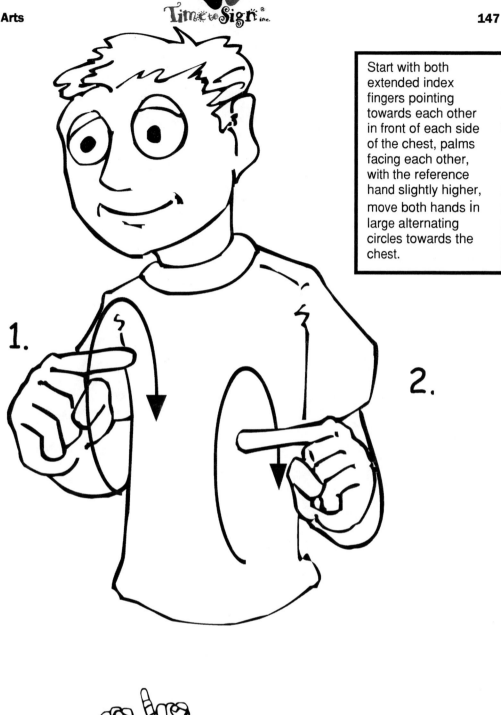

Start with both extended index fingers pointing towards each other in front of each side of the chest, palms facing each other, with the reference hand slightly higher, move both hands in large alternating circles towards the chest.

sign – seña

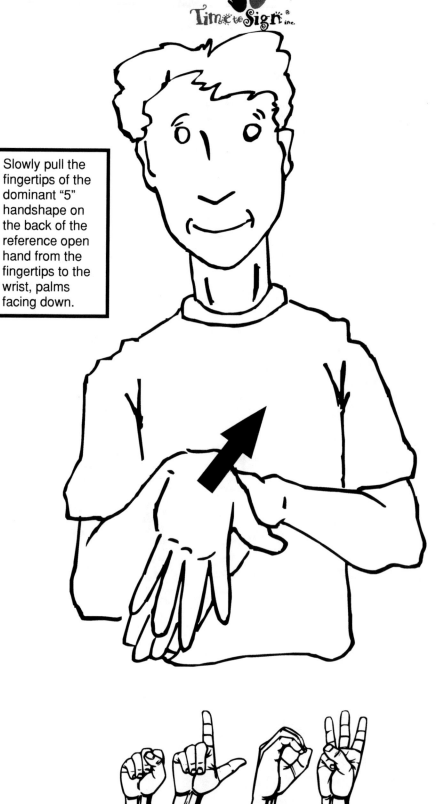

Slowly pull the fingertips of the dominant "5" handshape on the back of the reference open hand from the fingertips to the wrist, palms facing down.

slow - lento

Language Arts 149

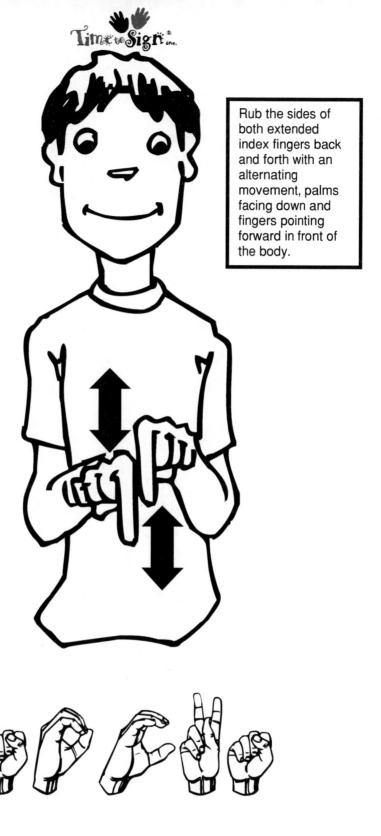

Rub the sides of both extended index fingers back and forth with an alternating movement, palms facing down and fingers pointing forward in front of the body.

socks – calcetín

Grasp the reference index finger with the fingers of the dominant "F" handshape and pull upward in front of the chest.

[Indicates being pulled out from the ordinary]

special – especial

Language Arts

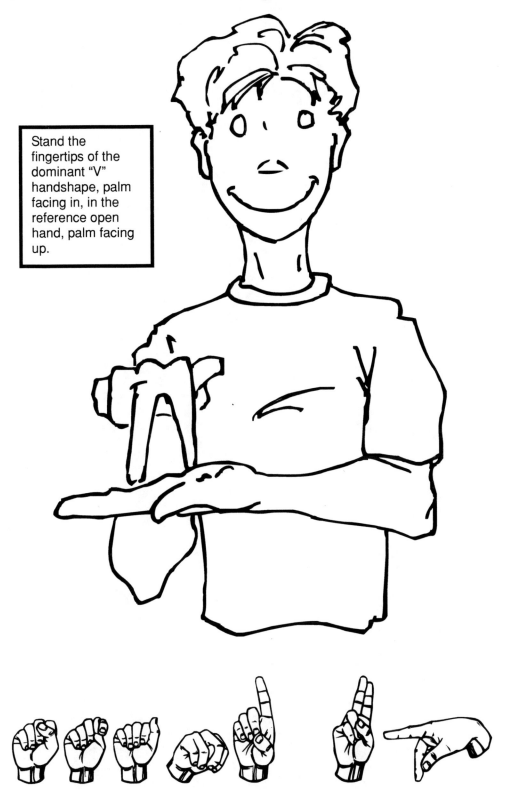

Stand the fingertips of the dominant "V" handshape, palm facing in, in the reference open hand, palm facing up.

stand up – de pie

Start with the extended little fingers of both "I" handshapes touching in front of the chest, palms facing in, move both hands outwards.

string - cordón

Language Arts

Start by crossing both "H" handshapes in front of the body, palm facing in, rotate the fingers forward and back with a double movement.

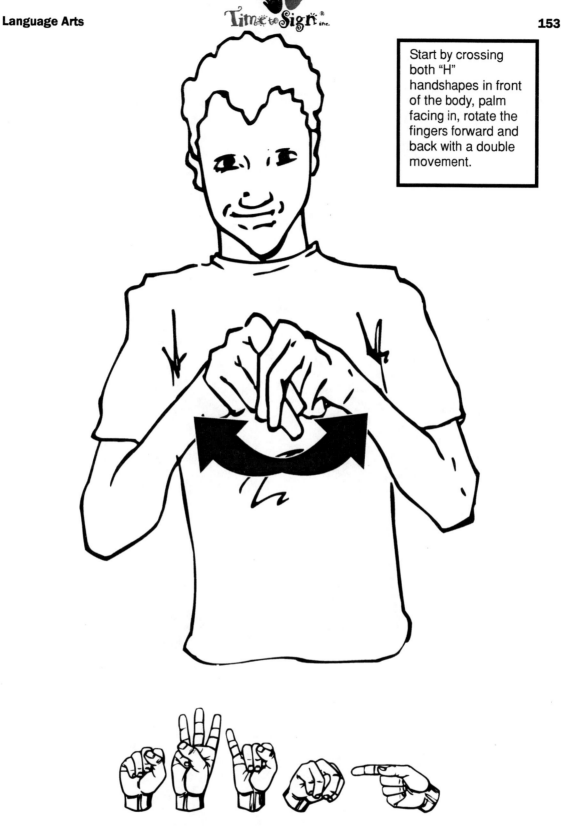

swing – columpio

Start with both curved "5" handshapes in the front of each side of the body, palms facing down, move the hands upwards towards the body while changing into "S" handshapes.

take – llevar

Language Arts 155

Push the little-finger side of the dominant "X" handshape, palm facing reference, forward with a repeated movement across the index-finger side of the reference "X" handshape, palm facing the dominant side.

tease – burlarse

Language Arts

Move the dominant index finger, held in front of the mouth,

tell – decir

Language Arts 157

Beginning with both flattened "O" handshapes held in front of the body, palms facing up and fingertips pointing toward each other, move the thumbs in circles across the other fingers.

texture - textura

Language Arts

Move the index finger away from the body towards a place, thing, person, etc.

there – allá

Language Arts

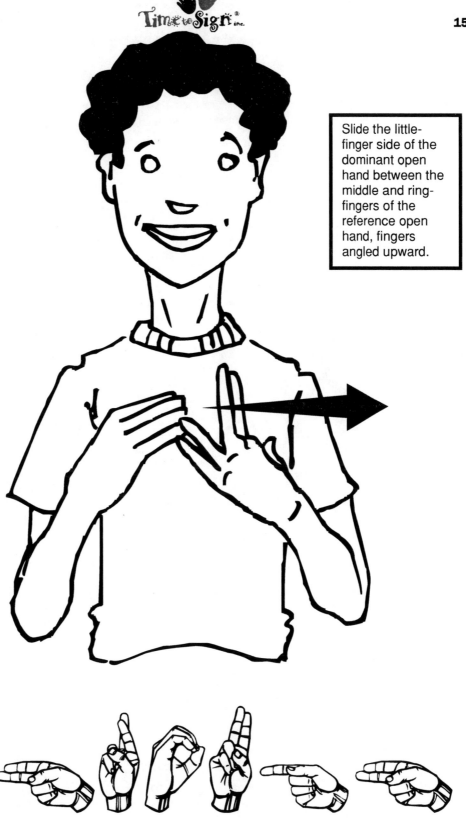

Slide the little-finger side of the dominant open hand between the middle and ring-fingers of the reference open hand, fingers angled upward.

through – algo a través de algo

Wiggle the dominant index finger by the dominant side of the abdomen, palm facing in.

[Indicates the action of tickling a person]

tickle – cosquilla

Language Arts

Bring the palms of both "A" handshapes together in front of the body, move the hands in a flat circle.

together – juntos

Touch the back of the reference hand with the dominant middle finger, other fingers extended, palms facing down.

no touch – no tocar
Shake your head no while making the touch sign.

touch – tocar

Language Arts 163

Move both "S" handshapes from in front of each side of the body, palms facing each other, downward, forward and out, then up slightly in simultaneous arcs.

try – probar

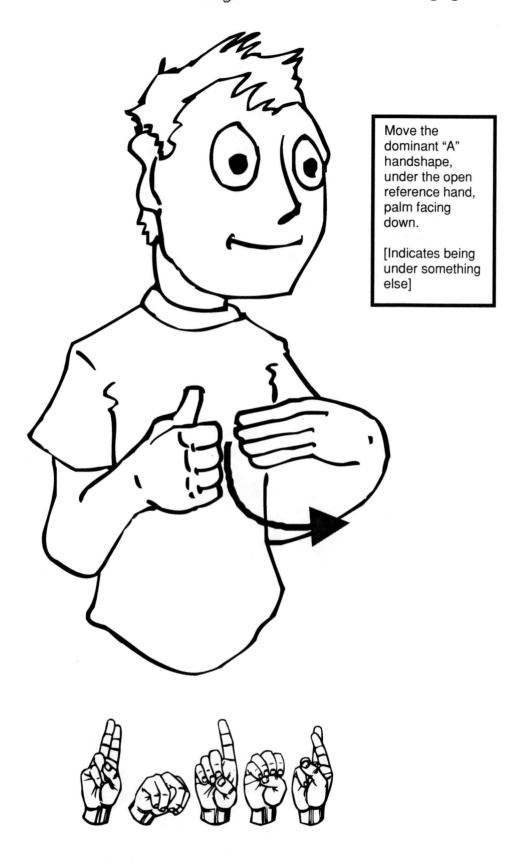

Move the dominant "A" handshape, under the open reference hand, palm facing down.

[Indicates being under something else]

under – debajo

Language Arts 165

Move the dominant "U" handshape, palm facing forward and fingers pointing up, in a repeated circle over the back of the reference "S" handshape, palm facing down, touching the heel of the dominant hand on the top of the reference hand as it passes.

use – usar

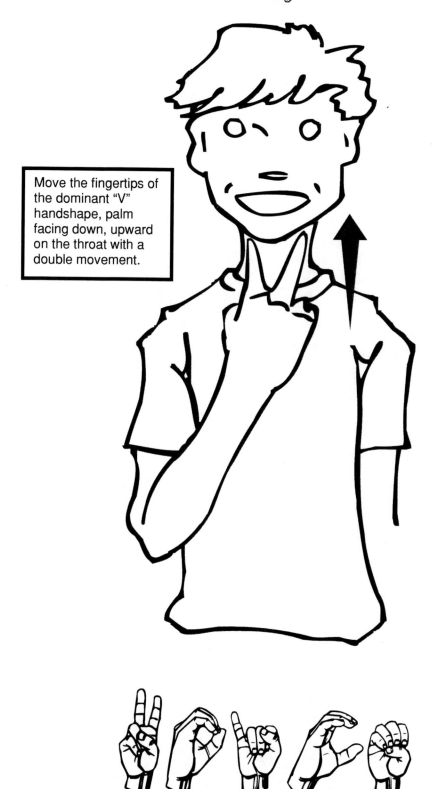

Move the fingertips of the dominant "V" handshape, palm facing down, upward on the throat with a double movement.

voice – voz

Language Arts

Beginning with both curved "5" handshape in front of the body, reference palm up in front of the dominant palm up, wiggle all fingers.

[As if asking for something]

wait - esperar

> Touch the extended dominant index finger, palm facing down, first to the dominant side of the chest and then to the reference side of the chest.

we – nosotros

Language Arts 169

Tap the heel of the dominant "S" handshape with a double movement on the back of the reference "S" handshape, palms facing down.

work – trabajo

Questions Signs

–

Señales De Preguntas

Language Arts 171

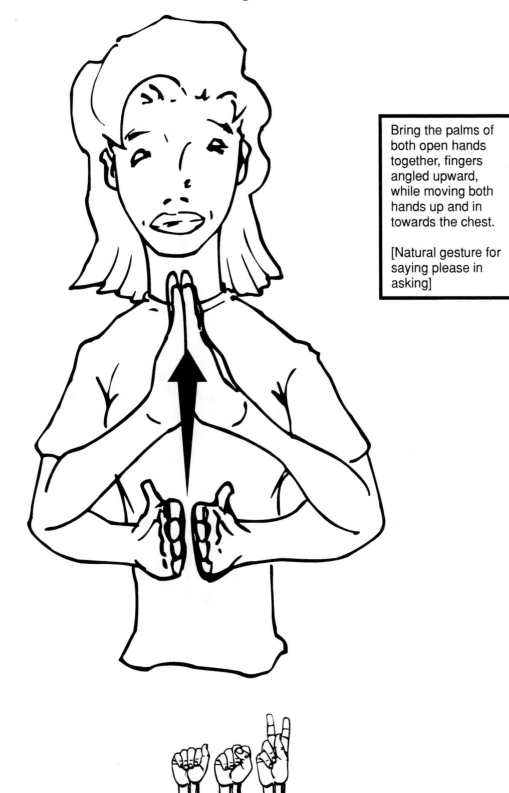

Bring the palms of both open hands together, fingers angled upward, while moving both hands up and in towards the chest.

[Natural gesture for saying please in asking]

ask - preguntar

Beginning with the knuckles of both curved hands touching in front of the chest, palms facing down, twist the hands upward and forward, ending with the fingers together pointing up and the palms facing up.

how - cómo

Language Arts

Start with the extended dominant index finger in front of the dominant shoulder, move the dominant hand down with a curved movement while retracting the index-finger, then extending it again at the bottom of the curve.

[As if drawing a question mark in the air]

question - preguntar

Language Arts

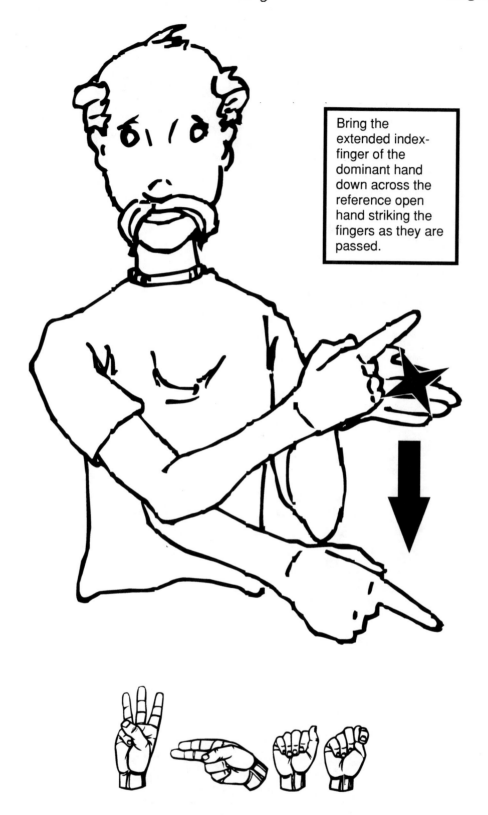

Bring the extended index-finger of the dominant hand down across the reference open hand striking the fingers as they are passed.

what - qué

Language Arts 175

Move the extended index-finger of the dominant hand in an arc to touch the extended index-finger of the reference hand in front of the reference hand side of the body.

when - cuando

Copyright © 2008 Time to Sign, Inc.

Hold up the dominant index finger, in front of the same shoulder, and shake the hand back and forth quickly, palm facing forward.

where - donde

Language Arts  177

With the thumb of the modified "C" handshape touch the chin, palm facing reference side, bend the index-finger up and down with a double movement.

who – quien

Copyright © 2008 Time to Sign, Inc.

178 Language Arts

Start with the dominant bent "5" handshape touching the forehead and then move the hand down as it becomes a "Y" handshape, palm facing in.

why - por qué

Alphabet Handouts - Alfabeto

Copyright © 2008 Time to Sign, Inc.

Alphabet Handout

Language Arts

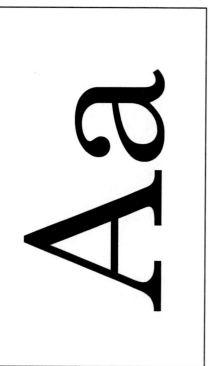

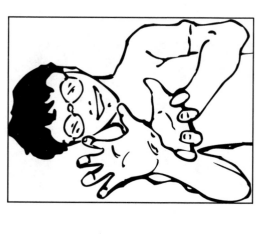
alligator - cocodrilo

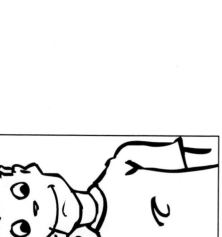
apple - manzana

airplane – aeroplano

ant - hormiga

www.timetosign.com

Copyright © 2008 Time to Sign, Inc.

Alphabet Handout

B b

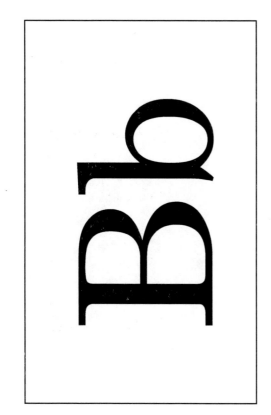

www.timetosign.com

bear - oso

book - libro

banana - plátano

bath - bañar

Language Arts

181

Copyright © 2008 Time to Sign, Inc.

Alphabet Handout

Language Arts

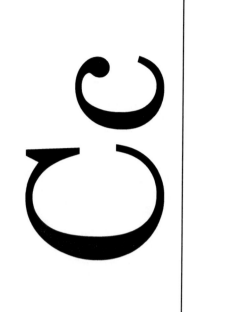

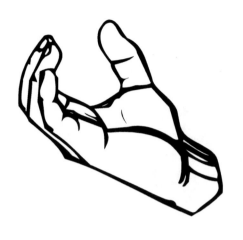

cold - frío

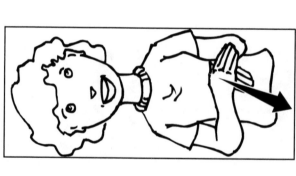
clean - limpiar

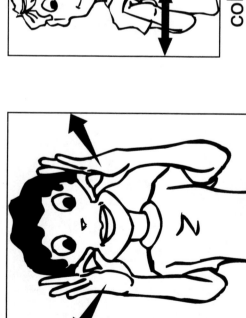
cat - gato

cow - vaca

www.timetosign.com

Copyright © 2008 Time to Sign, Inc.

Alphabet Handout

Dd

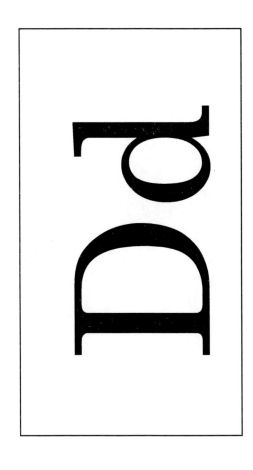

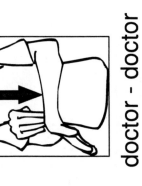

dance - baile

doctor - doctor

duck - pato

down - abajo

www.timetosign.com

Alphabet Handout

Language Arts

Ee

elephant - elefante

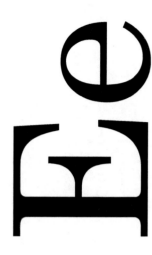

eat - comer

Easter - Pascua

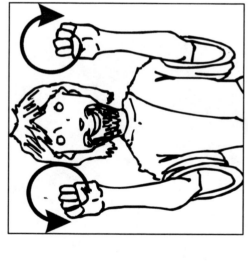

eggs - huevos

www.timetosign.com

Alphabet Handout

Ff

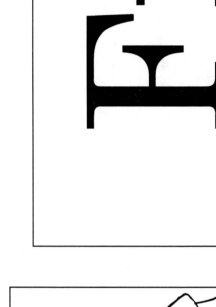

fish - pez

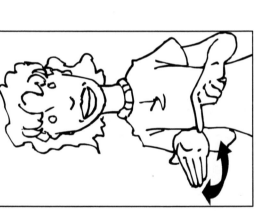

farm - granja

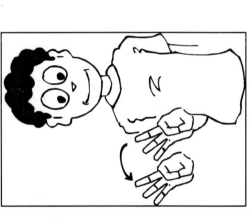

French fry – papas fritas

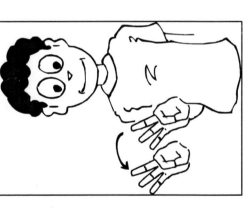

frog - rana

www.timetosign.com

Language Arts

Alphabet Handout

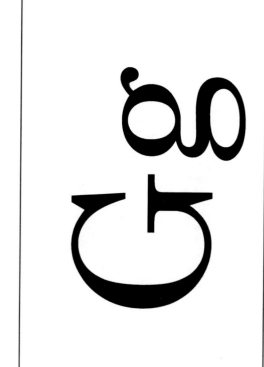 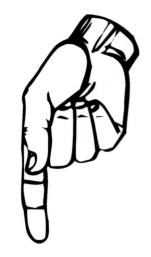

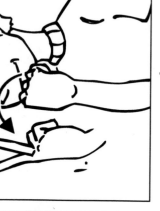

go - irse

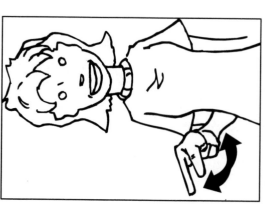

goat - cabra

green - verde

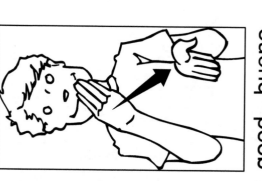

good - bueno

Alphabet Handout

Hh

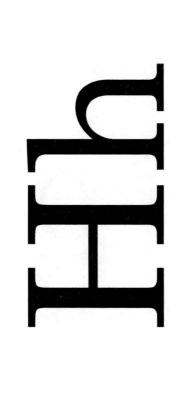
hot – caliente

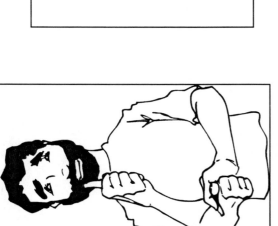
hide - esconderse

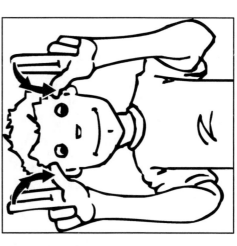
horse - caballo

home - hogar

Language Arts

www.timetosign.com

Copyright © 2008 Time to Sign, Inc.

Alphabet Handout

Language Arts

Ii

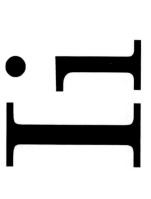

I - yo

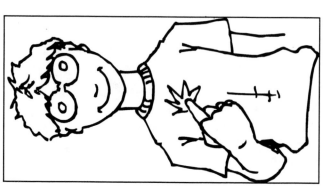

I love you – te quiero

ice cream - helado

www.timetosign.com

Alphabet Handout

Jj

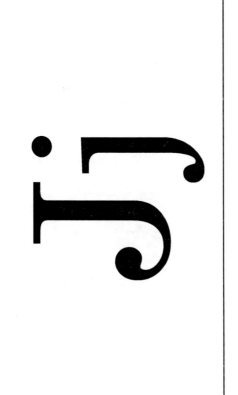
juice - jugo

jaguar - jaguar

jump – brincar

www.timetosign.com

Language Arts

Language Arts

Alphabet Handout

Kk

kangaroo - canguro

king - rey

kiss - beso

kite - cometa

www.timetosign.com

Copyright © 2008 Time to Sign, Inc.

Alphabet Handout

Language Arts

191

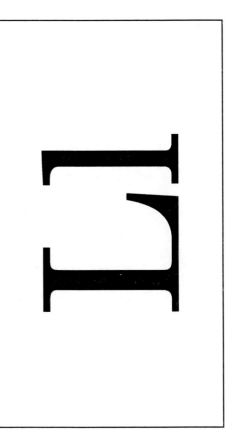

www.timetosign.com

llama - llama

lion - león

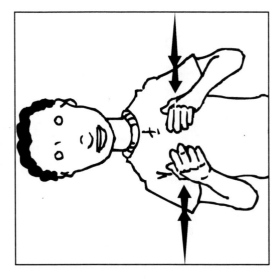

little - pequeño

lemon - limón

Copyright © 2008 Time to Sign, Inc.

Language Arts

Alphabet Handout

Mm

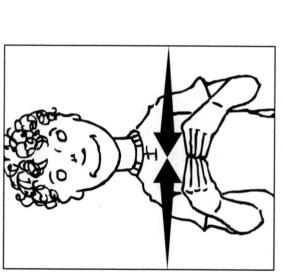

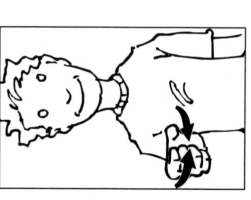

milk - leche

monkey - mono

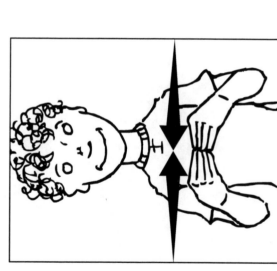

more - más

moon - luna

www.timetosign.com

Copyright © 2008 Time to Sign, Inc.

Alphabet Handout

N n

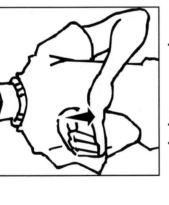
night - noche

nurse - enfermera

nice - amable

no - no

www.timetosign.com

Alphabet Handout

Language Arts

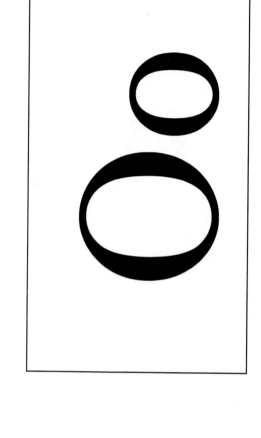

octopus - pulpo

off - lejos

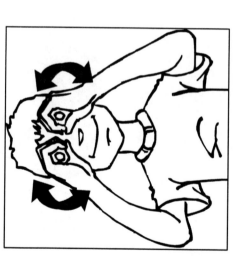

owl - buho

orange - naranja

www.timetosign.com

Copyright © 2008 Time to Sign, Inc.

Alphabet Handout

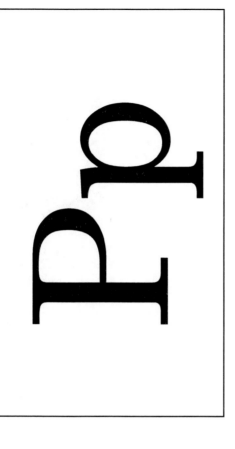

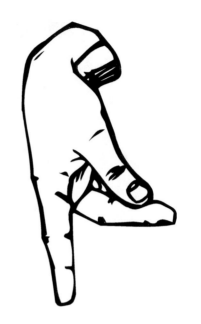

www.timetosign.com

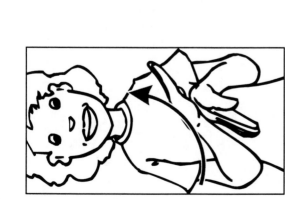

paper – papel

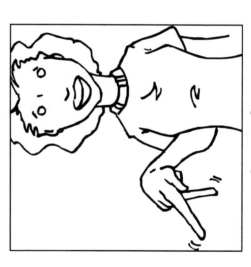

pretzel – galleta salada

please – por favor

purple – púrpura

Language Arts

195

Copyright © 2008 Time to Sign, Inc.

Language Arts

Alphabet Handout

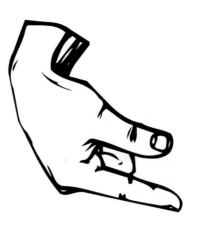

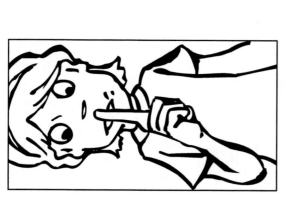

quiet - silencio

question - pregunta

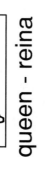

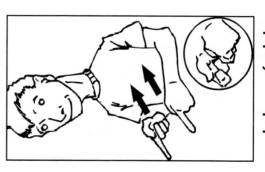

queen - reina

quick - rápido

www.timetosign.com

Copyright © 2008 Time to Sign, Inc.

196

Alphabet Handout

R r

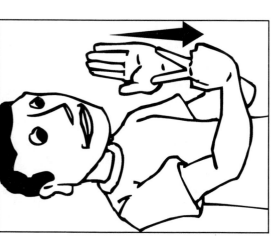
read - leer

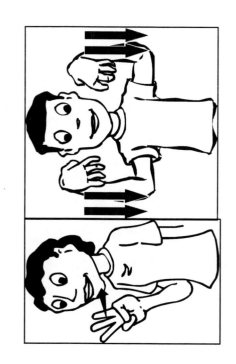
rain - lluvia

rabbit - conejo

rocket – cohete

www.timetosign.com

Copyright © 2008 Time to Sign, Inc.

Alphabet Handout

Ss

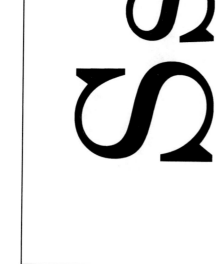
shark - tiburón

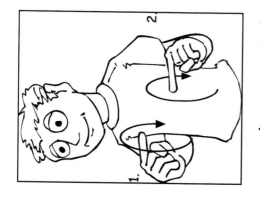
sign - señal

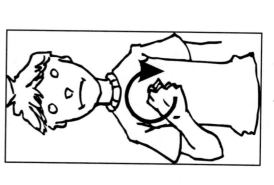
sorry – lo siento

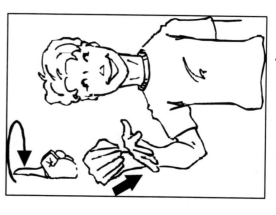
sun - sol

Alphabet Handout

Tt

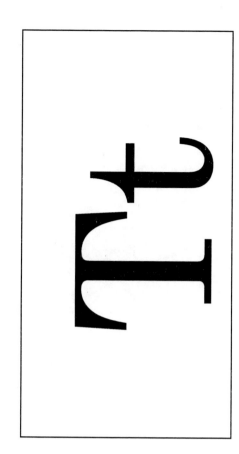

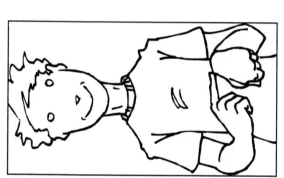

time - tiempo

tiger - tigre

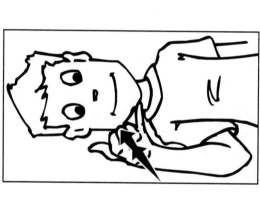

telephone - teléfono

toy – juguete

www.timetosign.com

Copyright © 2008 Time to Sign, Inc.

Language Arts

Alphabet Handout

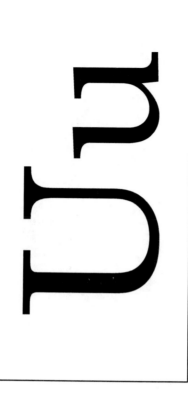

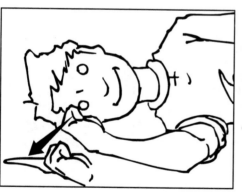
understand – entender

uncle - tío

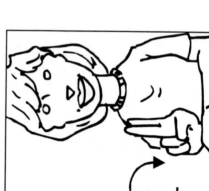
use – uso

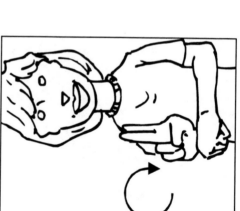
up - arriba

www.timetosign.com

Copyright © 2008 Time to Sign, Inc.

Alphabet Handout

Vv

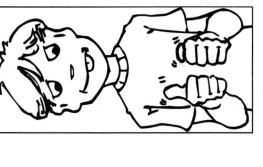
video game – juego de video

violin - violín

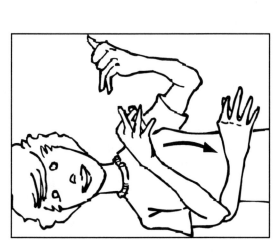
vegetable - vegetal

voice - voz

Language Arts

www.timetosign.com

Copyright © 2008 Time to Sign, Inc.

Language Arts

Alphabet Handout

W w

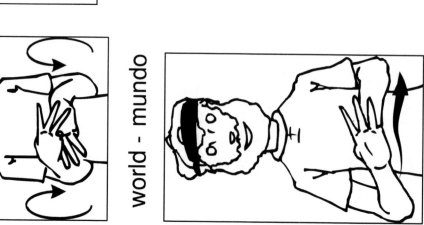

water - agua

world - mundo

wind - viento

whale - ballena

www.timetosign.com

Copyright © 2008 Time to Sign, Inc.

Language Arts

Alphabet Handout

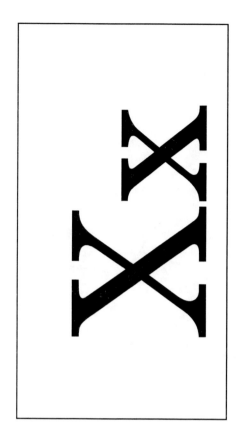

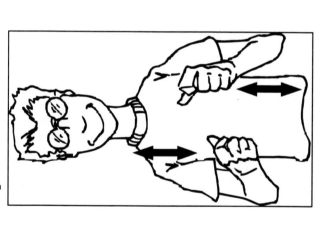

xylophone - xilofón

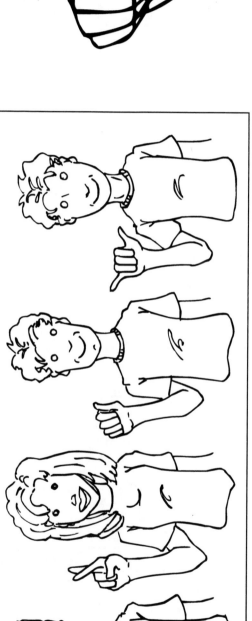

x-ray – rayo x

www.timetosign.com

Copyright © 2008 Time to Sign, Inc.

Language Arts

Alphabet Handout

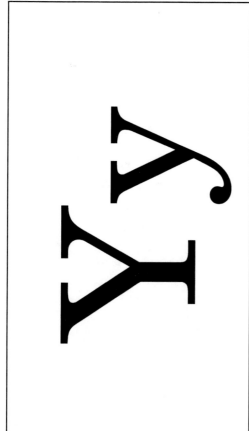

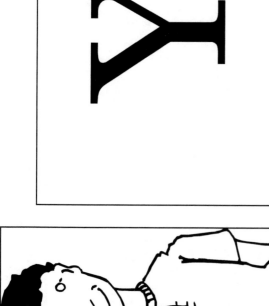

yellow - amarillo

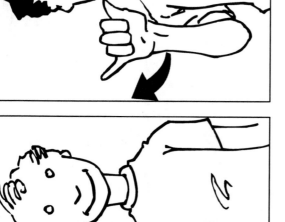

yes - sí

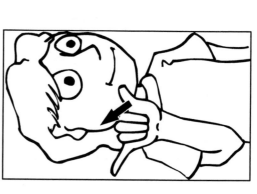

yesterday - ayer

www..timetosign.com

Alphabet Handout

zipper - cremallera

zebra - cebra

zoo - zoológico

www.timetosign.com

SIGN LANGUAGE HANDOUT

"The Alphabet Song" - Traditional

A - B - C - D - E - F - G,

H - I - J - K - L - M - N-

O - P,

Q - R - S, T - U - V,

W - X, Y and Z,

Now I know my A - B - Cs.

Next time won't you sign with me.

www.timetosign.com

Copyright © 2008 Time to Sign, Inc.

SIGN LANGUAGE HANDOUT - COLORS

brown – marrón

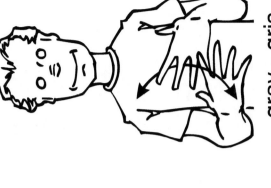
gray - gris

blue - azul

gold – oro

black – negro

colors - colores

www.timetosign.com

Copyright © 2008 Time to Sign, Inc.

SIGN LANGUAGE HANDOUT

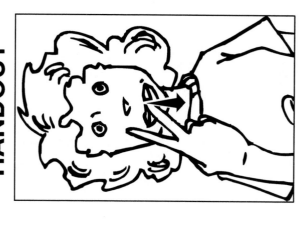

pink – color rosa

white – blanco

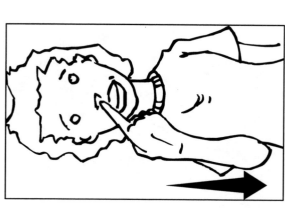

red – rojo

I'm a Little Valentine
- Original Author Unknown
(Tune of "I'm a little teapot")
I'm a little Valentine,
Red and white.
with ribbons and lace,
I'm a beautiful sight.
I can say I love you
On Valentines Day
Just put me in a envelope,
and give me away.

Language Arts

www.timetosign.com

Copyright © 2008 Time to Sign, Inc.

SIGN LANGUAGE HANDOUT – COLORS

peach – melocotón

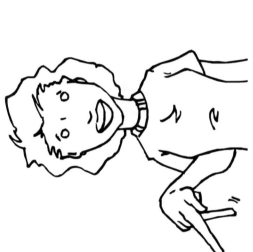
rainbow – arco iris

orange – naranja

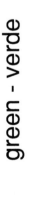
purple – púrpura

green – verde

pink – rosa

www.timetosign.com

Copyright © 2008 Time to Sign, Inc.

SIGN LANGUAGE HANDOUT – COLORS

Language Arts

silver – plata

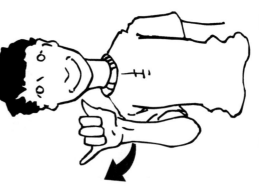

yellow – amarillo

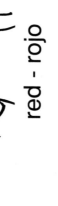

red – rojo

white – blanco

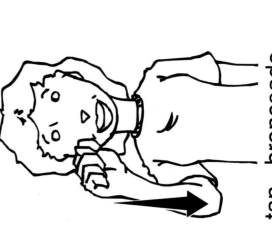

tan – bronceado

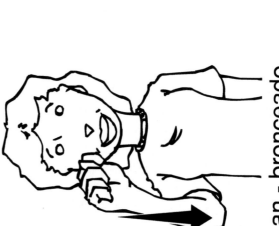

www.timetosign.com

Copyright © 2008 Time to Sign, Inc.

SIGN LANGUAGE HANDOUT

The More We Sign Together
- Traditional

The more we sign together, together, together,
The more we sign together, the happier we'll be.

'Cause your friends are my friends,
And my friends are your friends.

The more we sign together the happier we'll be.

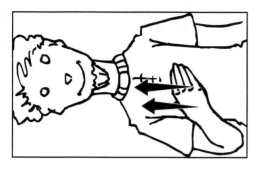

happier - feliz -

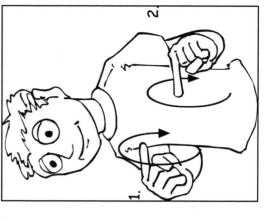

together - junto -

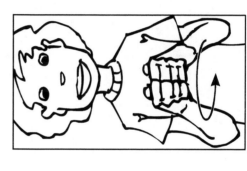

friends - amigos -

sign - seña -

www.timetosign.com

Copyright © 2008 Time to Sign, Inc.

Language Arts

SIGN LANGUAGE
HANDOUT - BENEFITS

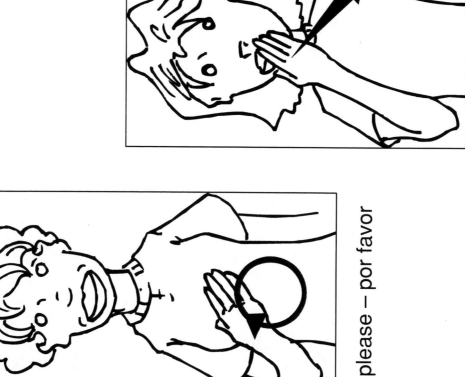

please – por favor

thank you - gracias

Benefits of Signing with Children

☞ Learning a second language makes additional language learning easier
☞ Raises communication awareness and abilities
☞ Enhances children's vocabulary and literacy skills
☞ Enhances children's' confidence and self-esteem
☞ Enhances fine and gross motor
☞ 2-sided brain activity that increases brain functioning
  o Visual right brain usage
  o Cognitive second language left brain usage
  o Creates additional connection or synapses in the brain coordination
☞ Enhances language acquisition

www.timetosign.com

SIGN LANGUAGE HANDOUT – QUESTIONS I

Language Arts

213

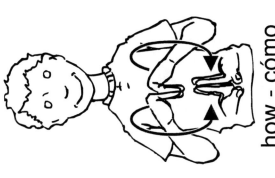
ask - preguntar

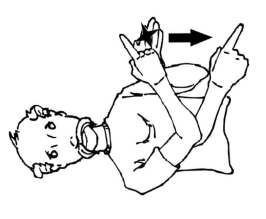
how - cómo

question - pregunta

what - qué

www.timetosign.com

Copyright © 2008 Time to Sign, Inc.

SIGN LANGUAGE HANDOUT – QUESTIONS II

Language Arts

where – donde

when – cuando

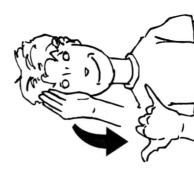

why – porqué

who – quien

www.timetosign.com

Index

Aa, 35, 180
airplane, 180
all, 62
alligator, 180
among, 63
ant, 180
apple, 180
around, 64
ask, 171, 213
away, 65

back, 66
ball, 67
balloon, 68
banana, 181
bath, 181
Bb, 36, 181
bear, 181
begin, 69
behind, 70
best, 71
bite, 72
black, 207
blow nose, 73
blue, 207
book, 181
bounce, 74
break, 75
brown, 207
brush hair, 76
brush teeth, 77
bubbles, 78

can't, 79
carry, 80
cat, 182
catch, 81
Cc, 37, 182
change, 82
clean, 182
coat, 83
cold, 182
colors, 207
congratulations, 84
cow, 182

dance, 85, 183
Dd, 38, 183
diaper, 86
dirty, 87
do, 88
doctor, 183
don't, 89
down, 183

dream, 90
drop, 91
drum, 92
duck, 183

Easter, 184
eat, 184
Ee, 39, 184
Eggs, 184
elephant, 184
explain, 93

face, 94
fall down, 95
far, 96
farm, 185
fast, 97
Ff, 40, 185
fight, 98
finish, 99
fish, 185
French Fry, 185
friends, 211
frog, 185
fun, 100

gentle, 101
Gg, 41, 186
go, 186
go on, 102
goat, 186
gold, 207
good, 186
gray, 207
great, 103
green, 186, 209
group, 104

happier, 211
hard, 105
have, 106
her, 107
here, 108
hers, 109
Hh, 42, 187
hide, 110, 187
him, 107
his, 109
home, 187
horse, 187
hot, 187
how, 172, 213

I, 111, 188

I love you, 188
ice cream, 188
Ii, 43, 188

jaguar, 189
Jj, 44, 189
journey, 112
juice, 189
jump, 113, 189

kangaroo, 190
king, 190
kiss, 190
kite, 190
Kk, 45, 190

lemon, 191
light, 114
like, 115
lion, 191
little, 191
Ll, 46, 191
llama, 191

make, 116
march, 117
me, 111
meet, 118
milk, 192
mine, 119
Mm, 47, 192
monkey, 192
moon, 192
more, 192
my, 119

near, 120
new, 121
nice, 193
night, 193
Nn, 48, 193
no, 193
nose, 122
not, 123
nurse, 193

octopus, 194
off, 124, 194
old, 125
on, 126
Oo, 49, 194
orange, 194, 209
others, 127
over, 128

owl, 194

paper, 195
passed, 129
peach, 209
peek-a-boo, 130
people, 131
person, 132
pink, 208, 209
play, 133
please, 195, 212
Pp, 50, 195
pretty, 134
pretzel, 195
problem, 135
purple, 195, 209

Qq, 51, 196
queen, 196
question, 173, 196, 213
quick, 97, 196
quiet, 136, 196

rabbit, 197
rain, 197
rainbow, 209
read, 197
ready, 137
red, 208, 210
rocket, 197
rough, 138
Rr, 52, 197
runaway, 139

said, 140
scream, 141
search, 142
see, 143
shark, 198
shine, 144

shoes, 145
show, 146
sign, 147, 198, 211
silver, 210
slow, 148
socks, 149
soft, 101
sorry, 198
special, 150
Ss, 53, 198
stand up, 151
Stand Up, 151
start, 69
string, 152
String, 152
sun, 198
swing, 153
Swing, 153

take, 154
Take, 154
tan, 210
tease, 155
telephone, 199
tell, 156
texture, 157
thank you, 212
there, 158
through, 159
tickle, 160
tiger, 199
time, 199
together, 161, 211
touch, 162
toy, 199
try, 163
Tt, 54, 199

under, 164, 200
understand, 200

up, 200
use, 165, 200
Uu, 55, 200

vegetable, 201
video game, 201
violin, 201
voice, 166, 201
Vv, 56, 201

wait, 167
water, 202
we, 168
whale, 202
what, 174, 213
when, 175, 214
where, 176, 214
white, 208, 210
who, 177, 214
why, 178, 214
wind, 202
work, 169
world, 202
Ww, 57, 202

x-ray, 203
Xx, 58, 203
xylophone, 203

yellow, 204, 210
yes, 204
yesterday, 204
you, 107
yours, 109
Yy, 59, 204

zebra, 205
zipper, 205
zoo, 205
Zz, 60, 205